TOUCHING GROUND

GENEVIEVE MCKAY

STONEPONY STUDIOS

CHAPTER 1

"Good, Astrid, now slow him down without losing impulsion; let him sink into those hocks and carry himself. Remember that you're *collecting* his active energy, not syphoning it away. He needs to be thinking about going forward all the time."

I nodded slightly, concentrating too hard on Red's outline and the supple leather driving reins running between my fingers to answer in words.

Red's neck arched proudly, his back curved in a lovely bascule as he brought his shoulders off the wall and moved down the long side in a three-track shoulder-in. He mouthed the bit gently, his eyes soft and his ears floppy, working without tension.

"Nice, straighten and then ask for traverse, haunches-in."

I straightened Red for a few steps, letting him move forward, before stepping closer to his hip, asking him to curve his haunches inward until he was moving on four separate tracks, his shoulders still close to the rail and his haunches curled to the inside. It was a bit harder of a movement for him since he had to cross his legs to propel himself forward and sideways at the same time, so I knew not to ask him to stay in that position for very long.

"Good, straighten him again, and then send him forward down the long side and we'll ask him for a few half-steps down at the far end."

He powered happily down the ring, his short, glossy red mane bouncing as he moved and his tail flowing out behind him in a silky wave. I slowed him as we came through the corner and took a deep breath as Oona moved up beside me, her short lunge whip reaching out and brushing him lightly on his croup, the top of his haunches, and clucked softly under her breath.

Red's ears flicked toward her and he stepped up smartly. For a second there was more pressure on the reins than I liked and then he shifted his weight backward to do a few half-steps of what would one day in the future become a piaffe.

Oona believed in teaching horses the foundations of all the upper-level movements right from the beginning, first in-hand and then using long-lines or driving reins from the ground. That way, by the time they were strong enough and their muscles were developed enough, they would already know what was being asked of them later under saddle. It also allowed trainers and riders to see what areas their horses were naturally strong in and which movements that they liked best. It had been an eye-opening experience.

"Good boy, Red," I encouraged under my breath, and his ear flicked ever so slightly toward me in acknowledgement.

"Okay, that's enough. Off you go before he gets stuck. And for heaven's sake don't run over that sheep."

I sent a quick side-glance over to where Portia, the world's most disobedient sheep, was lounging halfway down the opposite side of the ring, placidly chewing her cud while she watched Red and I work. She was lying down with her forelegs crossed neatly in front of her watching our movements as if she were an instructor, too.

"Don't worry about getting up," I told her as Red trotted a few feet past her nose. She let out a half-hearted *baa* in answer but didn't move an inch. "And what did you do with Antonio? Did you lose him again?"

She bleated a second time and I shook my head, hoping that Antonio hadn't broken into the tack room again or was busy annoying someone in the aisle.

Over the winter I had somehow become the owner of Portia and her adorably awful lamb Antonio who I'd rescued from becoming lamb chops. They slept in Red's stall at night to keep him company and had become unofficial barn mascots. But they were a handful sometimes and were forever breaking out and showing up where they were least wanted. And Antonio was getting worse the older he got.

"Keep your focus, Astrid," Oona warned and I shook my head free of daydreams and concentrated on moving Red forward.

I hadn't liked Oona much when she'd first arrived at Home Farm to be the resident coach. She'd seemed very unfriendly in the beginning; she rarely smiled and it had been hard to read her facial expressions most of the time.

She was also a demanding teacher and most of her students were serious competitors, not like Red and I at all.

I'd been overwhelmed with all the chaos going on in my life at the time and hadn't been very interested in taking lessons. I hadn't wanted any more pressure to perform or win. I'd just wanted to hang out with my horse, hit the trails, and play around with the mounted archery course we'd built in the woods.

But instead of ignoring me, Oona had taken me under her wing and had started teaching Red and I in-hand work and long-lining, something I'd barely even heard of before. This past winter she'd also started giving me drawing and painting lessons once a week, which was amazing because she was a world-class artist. Her work was hanging in galleries all over the world.

"That's enough for today," Oona said, bringing me back to the present again. "Give him a walk and let him stretch out."

I brought Red down to a walk and he immediately stretched his neck out and down, snorting contentedly.

"You worked hard, buddy," I told him. "But probably not as hard as I did."

I swiped the back of my hand across my dusty, sweaty forehead and tried to catch my breath. I swore that I got more of a workout than Red did when we schooled with the long-lines. I had to be on the move the whole time in order to keep up with him and I had to stay focused every single second. It was fun but definitely not relaxing.

"That was nice, Astrid. He's coming along well. You must be pleased."

"Yes, thanks so much for teaching me all this stuff. I'm having fun."

"You're welcome, now cool him out and get that bad sheep out of my ring before Linda's lesson. You know how fussy she is."

"I will, and thank you."

I coiled up the driving reins and unclipped one side from Red's bit, scratching his neck and telling him what a superstar he was.

He snorted happily and rubbed his nose on my arm before sniffing gently at my pockets where he knew his reward was stashed.

"Yes, there's something in there for you. I didn't forget."

As soon as I reached into my pocket to find a treat, Portia let out a loud, indignant *baa* and leapt to her feet, waddling toward us as fast as she could go. Her normally beautiful black and white coat was completely brown on one side from lying in the dirt. Even one half of her face was covered, including her eyelashes.

"No, you get nothing," I told her, mock-glaring down in answer to her greedy expression. "You're bad for escaping your paddock in the first place. I don't know why you choose to break into the arena when you have a whole farm to explore."

Ignoring my tone, she tilted her head to one side and looked up at me with her huge brown eyes. She knew exactly the right moves to make to extract treats from humans.

"Fine, just a small one, you're supposed to be on a diet. And you do realize that you're covered with dirt, right? Don't you even care about your appearance?"

She didn't. She tore the cookie out of my hand, barely chewing before she swallowed it and looked at me expectantly.

"No, you're cut off. Let's get you out of here before someone else sees you."

Most of the boarders actually loved the sheep and spoiled them rotten. And the majority of them thought it was hilarious when Portia and Antonio joined them in the ring for lessons. But there were a few riders, especially eccentric Linda, who were less than impressed and had complained loudly to Hilary and Oona on a couple of occasions. Linda had even threatened to take her horse and move to another barn which, in my opinion, wouldn't have been that bad of a thing. But Hilary was still struggling financially and I knew she couldn't afford to lose boarders.

I had to admit that the sheep *were* getting out of hand. Antonio had even recently started *butting* people, horses, and equipment with his head. I'd caught him butting Linda's Mercedes the other day but luckily nobody else had been around to witness it. I was pretty sure it was his way of playing but the older he got the more it hurt and he didn't always listen when he was told to stop. I couldn't imagine what he'd be like when he was a full grown three hundred pound ram like his father Hamlet.

Luckily, my aunt had agreed to take him up to her ranch to permanently join her own flock of sheep this summer, otherwise, I think Hilary would have kicked all of us out.

"Come on, Portia, let's go," I said, reaching down to grasp her leather collar in one hand to make sure she didn't bolt back into the ring. "We don't have much time before..."

I broke off as the door rolled back with a rumble and Linda stood there frowning at me beside her towering warmblood Baloo. She wore a pinched expression on her face and she drew back in distaste to let us pass as if owning a sheep was contagious.

"Hi, Linda," I said politely as we hurried by, "have a good lesson."

"Yes, thank you," she said in her clipped voice, looking down over her nose as Portia passed her. "I suppose I will."

I didn't take it personally. Linda was like that to everyone. She hated noise and young people and disorderly sheep. There actually wasn't much that she *did* like in life besides Baloo. Although she hadn't shown that very well when she'd first arrived.

She fussed over that horse all the time, getting him regular massages, chiropractors, and psychic readings. She fed him only the most expensive, trendy feeds and insisted that his stall had about two feet of bedding in it at all times. But she'd also ridden him with so many gadgets on his head that he could hardly breathe. She'd used sharp spurs to send him forward into her hard grip on the reins and had believed that his over-bent head carriage and hollow back was the sign of an obedient dressage horse.

I didn't know the name of the coach she'd ridden with before, but I really hoped that I never met the person who'd told her that riding a horse like that was okay. Baloo had arrived at our barn anxious, depressed, and afraid of his own shadow. And it was only because he was a nice horse that he hadn't bucked Linda off or refused to have anything more to do with riding at all.

Gradually, over the long winter, Oona had carefully restored their partnership, stripping away the gadgets one by one and teaching Linda to have the secure seat and steady hands that Baloo needed.

I hadn't been able to watch their lessons since Linda hated an audience but I'd watched her ride him on her own in the big outdoor ring and there had been miles of improvement.

I walked Red slowly up and down the gravel driveway in the spring sunshine while Portia grazed nearby. There was no sign of Antonio so I had my fingers crossed that he was just peacefully off grazing somewhere on his own. I strolled along, thinking dreamily back over my lesson when my phone began to ring.

"Hey," I said excitedly, "I'm glad it's you. We worked on the half-steps again today and..."

"Astrid," Rob interrupted, "Possum sold."

"Oh." I stopped, my heart constricting painfully. Possum was one of the project horses that my boyfriend Rob had been selling for my Aunt Lillian. She'd been sent down with a load of ranch horses from the interior and had quickly become Rob's favourite.

We'd always known that Possum was for sale but that hadn't stopped him from growing steadily more attached to her over the winter. Nobody had shown any interest in buying her so far so he'd had a whole season of competitions planned ahead for her.

"I'm so sorry."

"It's all right, I just thought you should know. The vet check was yesterday and the deal just went through this morning. They're picking her up after lunch."

"Wow, that's so soon," I said, feeling tears prickle at the edge of my eyes. I would probably never get to see her again. I wouldn't even get to say goodbye. "Would you like to come over for a trail ride this afternoon? If you bring Artimax I can come with you. And you should stay for dinner."

"Yeah, actually, that would be great. My dad has meetings tonight anyway but he already said he could drop me off."

"Well, then you definitely have to come."

"Right, see you this afternoon then."

He hung up abruptly without saying goodbye and I stared worriedly down at my phone. It wasn't like easy-going Rob to sound so sad. He normally shook things off and took all life's bumps in stride. And he'd worked with quite a few sales horses before so it wasn't like losing them was a new thing.

Possum had been different, though. She was smart and hard-working and had taken to cross-country like a duck to water. She was one of those horses who always tried everything the rider asked and never said no. She was fearless and fun, and we'd been surprised that nobody had been interested in her before.

"Well, I guess someone is interested now, hey Red?" I said out loud with a sigh. I felt his chest to make sure he was cool and dry. "At least I don't have to worry about you being sold. You're with me forever."

Antonio was, by some miracle, still asleep in the paddock when I got back. I took Red's tack off and gave him a final brushing before slipping on his halter and lead and heading out to the pasture.

I had to dump some grain in a bucket to distract the sheep long enough for me to escape. Neither of them liked being locked up and it was becoming more and more difficult to get Red out of the paddock without them following.

"Come on, buddy, you can spend the rest of the day out in the field with your friends," I told him.

I led him down the driveway to the lower pasture on the left and sent him through the gate, watching with satisfaction as he strolled out to meet his friends. We'd gotten a bunch of new boarders in the year before and Red had taken a liking to the big pinto gelding named Oreo. They spent most of their free time grazing together and it was always fun to watch them napping side by side out in the field.

It was one of the rare days when I didn't have a full schedule. My barn chores were done, the archery range was closed for the weekend since my coach, Earl, was away on holidays and I'd already had my lesson with Red.

I'd done my daily prep work for my school exams that morning. They were coming up in a couple of weeks but I wasn't panicking. I was pretty sure that I'd do well enough. I was good at school, although I didn't love it, and I wasn't the type to stress about getting top grades as long as I passed everything. I got As in the things I liked and As or Bs in the things I didn't like, and that was good enough.

Up until recently, my plans had always revolved around going to the Olympics for archery. That's what my dad had expected of me, and what I'd been certain I'd wanted for myself.

But now I wasn't so sure.

I hung Red's halter and lead on the gate and walked slowly up the hill, back past the row of paddocks and attached wooden shelters where Red and a few of the boarders lived, past the indoor and the fancier barn where the rest of the horses were boarded and up toward the house.

The road curved steadily upward and I paused when I reached the upper sheep pasture to lean on the fence and catch my breath.

This was where the actual working sheep lived, the ones who weren't pets but were instead meant to be eaten.

They were Hilary's dad's flock and Portia had originally come from there too. He had chickens, quail, and a huge vegetable garden. His project had been to grow as much of their own food as possible and to open a sustainable restaurant this summer, but he wasn't overly thrilled now with the idea of actually killing the animals he was raising.

At least I kept Portia and Antonio from being chops, I thought, reaching through the fence and scratching a friendly speckled lamb who'd trotted up to be petted. Being around farm animals non-stop was enough to almost turn me into a vegetarian. Almost. Honestly, if I didn't love food so much…

My thoughts broke off as a small brown dog hurtled toward me, spraying gravel in all directions.

"Hey, Caprice,' I said happily as she landed at my feet, grinning up at me with her tongue out, a pink rubber ball clamped between her teeth.

"Oh you want me to throw this, do you?"

She spit the saliva-covered ball out and leapt backward in preparation, staring up at me expectantly and then back at the ball again and then back to me, her eyes wide with excitement.

I picked the slimy thing up gingerly between two fingers and then threw it as far as I could in the direction of the house, laughing as the little poodle sprang away as fast as she could, yapping her high-pitched excited bark the whole time she ran.

Maybe I'll actually sit down and read a book, I thought, suddenly wondering what I'd even do with a whole afternoon to myself. I usually kept myself as busy as possible, either with farm work, studying or archery. Too much time alone with my own thoughts was dangerous.

I'll read that book on horse psychology, I told myself firmly, *that will keep my occupied.*

But already my thoughts were drifting to the thing I tried to avoid the most. My crazy, unstable parents and their sickly new baby. My little sister.

She'd been born two months before her scheduled due date and my step mom, Marion, had not had an easy delivery.

Underweight and underdeveloped, my sister had spent the first few months of her short life hooked up to tubes and monitors in an ICU ward up in Alaska where they lived.

She hadn't been expected to make it. My parents hadn't even given her a proper name yet because every moment had seemed like it would be her last. Which I thought was awful because she still deserved a name no matter how short a time she stayed on earth.

Anyway, I'd spent the last few months torn between gnawing guilt and agonizing worry. Even though I'd cut my parents out of my life almost completely, I still cared about them and I certainly didn't want anything bad to happen to an innocent baby.

Logically I knew that none of this had been my fault but the guilt had a way of getting its claws into me anyway. I'd made no secret that I thought that it was a bad idea for them to have another child in the first place. They had been terrible parents to me and I hated to think of another child having to go through all that. And even though it was completely irrational, a part of me couldn't help thinking that it was my lack of love that had reached out and caused the baby to get sick in the first place. Like maybe if she'd felt *wanted* she'd be strong enough to live.

Anyway, she didn't die. Despite everything stacked against her, she was now two months old and her prognosis had been upgraded from grim to cautiously optimistic.

Marion had even sent me a photo of her in her little ventilated crib. Honestly she looked like a wrinkled little alien but my heart had still thrummed with gratitude that she was still, at least temporarily, alive.

Still, it was better for my nerves if I just avoided thinking about any of them at all.

I sat down resolutely on my bed with my horse psychology book spread out in front of me and Caprice curled up in my lap. I'd grabbed a pad of paper and a pen so I could take notes, just like I was studying for a test.

When I concentrated hard enough the world outside my room just seemed to disappear.

CHAPTER 2

Rob didn't arrive with the horses until late that afternoon.

We rode through the woods in the direction of the beach, our bows slung over our shoulders and our feet dangling free from the stirrups.

This spring had been another hot one and my favourite time of day was that turning-point moment when the heat leaked out of the air and was replaced by the fresher, cooler ocean breezes.

Rob had greeted me with a tight hug and a kiss like usual but we'd been surrounded by boarders and riders the whole time we were unloading and tacking up the horses so we'd hardly had a second alone to talk. Rob was popular with everyone and people seemed to gravitate toward him wherever he went, asking him questions about horses or just stopping to chat. He was just the type of guy you wanted to be around.

Once our ride started, he'd had to focus all his attention on his big baby horse, Ferdi, who could still be silly sometimes when he felt like it even though he was a fully grown seven-year-old. Far too old for those shenanigans, in my opinion.

It took him a few minutes to settle down and then he went

peaceably enough on a loose rein. Ferdi had been on these trails hundreds of times and probably could have done the entire ride by himself if given the chance.

Artimax was a perfect gentleman, of course. He was my favourite horse, next to Red, and even though he'd started out with a few quirks when Rob had bought him, he was now a seasoned horse who just wanted to have fun and enjoy life with as little trouble as possible.

It wasn't until halfway through our ride, when we'd paused at the grass rise that overlooked the ocean, that I finally felt like it was the right time to mention Possum.

Both horses stood like statues, their eyes fixed on the water below. They lifted their noses and inhaled deeply, ears twitching. Even though every horse in the barn saw the ocean regularly they all seemed perpetually fascinated by the waves and every time we rode this way they would spend a few minutes snorting and puffing in excitement.

"I really am sorry about Possum, Rob," I said finally. "I hope it's a great home for her."

He was silent for a long time, staring down at Ferdi's arched neck rather than the vast sea stretching out in front of us. It had been a pointless statement anyway. Because as if Rob would ever sell a horse to a substandard home.

"Yeah," he said finally, sighing. "They're really nice. This couple bought her for their twelve-year-old boy. He's a good, quiet rider moving up from a pony he evented on locally for the last two years. They're retiring the pony at their house too, not selling him, so you can tell they love their horses. He has a solid dressage foundation so I think Possum will do really well there." He reached down and stroked Ferdi's neck absently. "It still sucks, though."

"It does," I agreed. "I felt that way about Ellie's new owners when they bought her, too. It was just so hard to think of her somewhere strange where I couldn't protect her."

He nodded and then reached out and squeezed my hand tightly for a moment before letting go.

"Come on," he said finally, "let's go shoot something."

He swung Ferdi around, up the path away from the beach, and then moved him into an easy canter. I let Artimax follow, leaving his reins on his neck.

I stretched my arms upward over my head and then out to the side, practicing swivelling from side to side, and looking backward over my shoulder without upsetting my balance. It was important that a mounted archer be able to trust their horse in all situations, letting them find their own way across the ground while the rider focused on the targets. It had to be a genuine partnership between horse and rider or it just wouldn't work.

Trusting just *any* horse wasn't something that came easily to me, though. Only with Red and Artimax could I let myself go like this, and that trust had been built up by working together for years.

Ahead of me, Rob had reached the first of our targets that we'd peppered throughout the wooded trail.

His back and shoulder muscles bunched beneath his t-shirt as he drew back his bowstring in an effortless move, his brow creased, his deeply tanned arm muscles rippling. His arrow twanged through the air and buried itself in the target with a thud.

"Easy, Artimax," I said, sitting up to slow him down a little as I set my sights on the bullseye.

I anchored my knuckles on my cheekbone for just as long as it took me to inhale and loose the arrow with a twang. I barely had time to watch it hit home before we were moving on to the next one.

This one was set higher in the trees, an upward shot on a bit of an angle and I anchored myself firmly in the saddle, leaning into my left stirrup for a second so I could hold firm. Hiss.

Thwack. The arrow sank deep into the lower half of the target. Not a bullseye but not a miss, either.

Rob launched his arrow into the double-sided one ahead of us, but I had a different strategy.

Wait for it, I told myself, as the target grew closer and closer. I let it pass by and then, at the last second, I stood in my stirrups, swivelled around backward and blasted an arrow right into the bullseye.

Ha, I congratulated myself, reaching down to pat Artimax's neck enthusiastically. It was my favourite shot. It took balance, flexibility, and a leap of faith that your horse wasn't going to do something stupid right at that moment when you were most vulnerable.

A year ago I wouldn't have been nearly so comfortable taking that shot.

Up ahead, I saw Rob draw Ferdi down to a trot as they headed uphill to the new section of the trail. The terrain wasn't as soft and sandy here so we had to keep an eye on our footing a little. Over the winter and spring, our archery course had steadily expanded. Instead of being cramped into one little area, it now followed a winding trail through the woods and we'd added quite a few targets. Hilary and her family hadn't been using this section of woods anyway so they hadn't cared that we'd created a trail. And Hilary's boyfriend Darius was into horse archery a bit so as soon as he got excited about helping she was all for it.

I shot a couple more easy targets but I could tell Artimax was getting tired.

"All done for today, boy?" I asked him, drawing him down to a walk. "That's okay, it's a long track and you're still working off your winter weight. You need to ease into it."

Rob was waiting for us up ahead in a little clearing. The fading light filtered down through the trees and speckled across his face and Ferdi's deep red coat, transforming them for a second into something wild and a little otherworldly. As if they'd sprung from the woods or out of one of Oona's paintings.

She was currently working on a "Horses in Myth" series and right then Rob could have been a young Mongolian warrior or an ancient tree spirit come to life.

A small smile played across his lips as I approached and he held out one hand to catch my attention.

"Look," he whispered, pointing quietly to a space above our heads.

I tilted my head back and almost jerked to the side. There above us, perched on the lower branches of a giant cedar, sat a family of very large, intimidating-looking owls. They stared down in absolute silence, taking us in with wide yellow eyes, their heads tilted, unblinking.

A shiver rippled over my skin and I moved Artimax quickly past them so they weren't directly over my head.

"Great horned owls," Rob said in the same quiet voice, "a whole family of them. They're beautiful."

They *were* beautiful. But there were also incredibly unnerving.

"I don't think they want us here," I said, feeling another shiver zig-zag down my spine. "We should go." I directed Artimax firmly down the trail, not looking back until Rob and Ferdi caught up with us.

"I can't believe you're afraid of owls," Rob laughed. "I would have never guessed it."

"Not afraid." I paused. "Maybe just a little creeped out. It felt like we were intruding on their family gathering or something."

"Weirdo," Rob said affectionately, making me laugh. "Owls aren't scary. In my culture, they're a symbol for wisdom, and for change. Sometimes big changes."

"Well, I definitely don't like big changes. I've had enough of those to last me a lifetime. And how are you calling me weird? You're way stranger than me." I stuck my tongue out at him.

"That is debatable. Hey, I forgot to tell you that your aunt

Lillian wants you to call her. I talked to her this morning when the family made the offer on Possum. She sounded excited about something but she wouldn't tell me what. She said she wanted to tell you first."

"Well, that sounds interesting. I hope nothing's wrong. I hope nothing happened to Folly … or to Quarry or ..."

My mind instantly began listing off all the awful things that might have happened to the people or horses that I'd left behind at the ranch.

"Of course it's nothing bad. I said she was excited not in the middle of a disaster."

"Well, I worry …"

"Yes, about everything, I know. Anyway, I'm sure you'll find out when you call her. She's happy that Possum sold. She wants to send me more horses."

"Well, I'm not surprised about that. How many?"

"I told her that I can't take more than two at a time. I'm sure she'd send me more if she could, though. It sounds like she has a lot of extra stock."

"Yeah." I frowned. That was one thing Aunt Lillian and I didn't see eye to eye on. She bred really fantastic horses, but she had so many new colts a year that the market couldn't keep up with them and she always had a surplus.

The super fancy ones often sold right away for big money as soon as they were weaned. Her top horses went to homes all over the world. But they couldn't *all* be top horses; the rest of them, the less fancy ones or the late bloomers, had to wait until the right home came along and sometimes that could take years. I felt that if she put a hold on the breeding for a few years then she might be able to catch up. But the foals were her favourite part of ranching and I didn't think anything would convince her to give it up.

"Hey," I said, suddenly remembering my own looming errand. "Did she ask you to go to the ranch and pick some out? I need to get Portia's lamb up there somehow soon; he's starting to be a lot of trouble. Hilary's going to kill me if he stays around much longer."

"Well, yeah, Lillian mentioned something about that. It sounds like she really wants you to visit."

"I'd love to go up there again. I miss it a lot. I haven't seen Folly or Quarry in over a year except for the pictures and videos that Liza sends me. Little Figaro is going to be half grown by the time I see him again."

Quarry had been the horse I'd loved most before I'd gotten Red. He'd belonged to my old coach Claudia and now he belonged to my friend and instructor, Liza. Folly had once, very briefly, been my horse but she had been way too much for me to handle. I'd made everyone happy when I'd gifted her to Liza. And Figaro had been an orphaned colt that Folly had taken under her wing when his own mother had died.

"A road trip would be fun," Rob said and I felt a surge of excitement, wondering if we'd be allowed to make the trip by ourselves.

"Would your dad let you drive the truck and trailer?"

"Um, no, I doubt it. I mean he trusts me and all, but I haven't had my licence very long. He would probably insist on coming along to supervise."

I laughed and ducked low in the saddle as Artimax navigated his way around a young tree that had partly fallen across our path.

"I wouldn't mind that, your dad is the best." Rob's dad was the kindest, most supportive parent that I knew. And he'd extended that kindness and concern to include me too when I'd run away from my parents.

He drove Rob to all sorts of lessons and horse shows and paid for almost everything although Rob helped him out by working in his office sometimes. It helped, of course, that Rob was pretty much a perfect son, too. He worked hard with the horses, got top grades, and helped work at his dad's construction and contracting company. He also stuck with eventing because his dad loved watching him compete, even though his real love was dressage.

"You're just sucking up because he buys you dessert all the time."

"Hey, that's not true. Okay, well maybe it's partly true. He does keep me stocked with a steady supply of fry bread."

One of their family friends was a chef who owned a food truck that focused on indigenous cuisine. They served all sorts of delicious food but what I was addicted to was the lightest, fluffiest, most delicious fry bread I'd ever tasted in my life. Sprinkled with cinnamon and sugar or filled with raspberry or chocolate, it was completely addicting and I could eat it all day long if left to my own devices.

"But, one way or another, a road trip would be fun. It would be good to get away and do something different."

"And maybe I could check on the archery team and see how they're doing. I haven't heard a lot of news from them lately."

When I'd lived at my aunt's, I'd helped to resurrect the local school archery team. We'd even built a range in an old abandoned dairy barn on the ranch property that now other people in the community used, too. They'd become quite competitive since I'd left and I was dying to see them in action.

Even though it was almost dusk, lessons were in full swing when we got back to the barn and the parking lot was crowded with cars. Two random children dressed in karate uniforms were playing tag on the grassy area in front of the barn, laughing and squealing at the top of their lungs.

Rabbit, my friend Pender's big thoroughbred, had come out into his paddock to investigate, hanging his big head over the fence and reaching out to nibble at them as they raced by. The little girl's flying pig-tails looked in immediate danger of being eaten.

The kids probably belonged to one of the riding students because clearly they knew nothing about how to act around horses. They veered suddenly off the grass and came straight toward us.

"No running around the horses," I called as the pig-tailed girl, who wasn't paying attention to where she was going at all, almost ran smack into Artimax's chest.

Her shriek was high-pitched enough to shatter glass. She skidded to a stop, looking way up at Artimax's nose with a shocked expression before backing hurriedly away a few steps. Her younger brother stopped a few feet away, his fists going up in a miniature karate stance as if he were about to launch himself at someone for scaring his sister.

"That horse almost ran me over," the girl said, her fear turning quickly into outrage. "He's dangerous."

She crossed her arms and sent me a deadly glare.

Wow, these two are feisty, I thought. Maybe karate wasn't quite the sport they needed. Maybe some yoga or meditation would do them good.

"Actually, you're lucky he's such a good horse. Another horse could have trampled you or spun around and kicked you with both hind legs when you surprised him like that. Do you know how much force a horse can exert when he kicks?"

"No." She looked sullenly down at the ground, her cheeks flushing with embarrassment.

"What about you?' I asked the younger boy who'd dropped his karate stance and had now sidled up to join his sister. He eyed up the horses nervously and then his gaze slid to my bow and the quiver still half-full of arrows. He shook his head and gulped loudly.

"Up to two thousand pounds per square inch. Do you know how many bones that could break? Or what if he kicked you in your face? Can you imagine what your parents would say?"

"Okay, sorry," the girl said with an exaggerated sigh, sounding like she at least partway meant it.

"That's fine, you can play out here as much as you like. There's lots of room to run around. Just pay attention to your surroundings so you don't get hurt. Horses are wonderful animals, but you need to respect them."

"Can I pet him?" the boy asked suddenly, edging closer to Artimax.

"Of course, stand right at his shoulder here and you can pet him. He's very friendly."

The boy moved to Artimax's shoulder and reached out tentatively, running his hand lightly across the horse's silky coat a couple times before stepping away.

"He's soft. Thanks, we've got to go." He grabbed his sister's hand and they took off at run toward the parking lot without looking back.

"Wow, look at you laying down the law," Rob said, laughing.

"Well, between the kids here and the kids at archery camp, I think I've lost all patience with them. They don't listen unless you're firm right from the beginning. Scaring them a little doesn't hurt, either. You should hear my speech about arrow safety. One of the parents told me that I gave her kid nightmares. Better that than a visit to the hospital, though."

We untacked and gave both horses a quick bath before leading them up to the orchard paddock at the top of the hill. Since Rob was staying for dinner that meant Artimax and Ferdi got to have some extra pasture time, too.

The house smelled amazing when we stepped inside. Mr. Ahlberg, who was Hilary's dad and my unofficial adopted father, was busy in the kitchen cooking up more food than one family could possibly eat. As per usual.

Every burner on the massive, commercial stove was covered in sauce pans and steaming pots and bubbling water.

"Um, can we do anything to help?" I asked, looking around at the chaos with a sigh. I had the feeling that it would be me, Rob, and Hilary who would be cleaning all this mess up after dinner.

"Right, you two, you're just in time. Wash your hands, you're on salad duty," Mr. Ahlberg said. "We've had a bit of a change of plans; Darius and his uncle will be here in a half hour and they're bringing dessert. Hilary was supposed to be helping but she's upstairs getting ready instead. I'm afraid she's in a bit of a panic."

"Ah," I said, going to the fridge and pulling out ingredients. "Apple and cheese okay?"

"Sure, whatever you like," he mumbled peering down at the simmering contents of a saucepan.

I normally wasn't much of a lover of leafy-greens but I'd become addicted to these spinach salads Mr. Ahlberg made with cubed apples and cheese. The whole thing would be sprinkled with dried cranberries, nuts, and sunflower seeds, and drenched in a ranch dressing. Delicious.

Rob took care of dicing the apples into tiny squares and I put the washed and dried spinach in a huge metal serving bowl and started on cubing the cheese.

"So, uh, Darius's uncle is really coming over? That's a surprise."

"Yes, a last minute one," Mr. Ahlberg said, sending me a wink. "He's coming to check us all out, I suppose."

"Poor Darius. Poor Hilary."

"Oh, they'll be alright. They're both strong minded, independent people. I don't think a cranky old uncle will stop either of them from doing much of anything."

He was right of course. Hilary and Darius had been dating determinedly for over a year, despite the difference in their ages, temperaments, and life experiences. And despite the concerns of Hilary's parents or Darius's uncle. For the two of them, it had been love at first sight.

But Darius really loved and respected his uncle too, and it was important to him that Nabil approved of their relationship eventually. He owed his uncle his life after all. Nabil had lobbied hard to bring Darius to Canada after the rest of their family had been killed by bombs in Syria. Darius had been away at boarding school in England when it had happened, and overnight he had found himself an orphan and a penniless refugee without a country of his own to go back to.

It was only because Darius was a gifted athlete that he'd gotten permission to move to Canada so quickly but even then, it had taken over a year to get him safely home. It had taken all the efforts of his coach at boarding school, Nabil, and the local Squash club here to keep him from getting deported back to Syria where he would have surely been killed or forced to fight.

So he owed his uncle a lot. But the fact that Nabil was visiting Hilary's family now was a positive sign that he was thawing a little.

The rich smell of cooking food, and the rhythmic chop, chop of our knives on the wooden boards and the feeling of Rob's shoulder next to mine was such a good, comforting feeling that I wanted to capture it like a video clip and keep it locked away so I could take it out and look at it later.

But then Mr. Ahlberg sent a spoon clattering loudly to the floor and the spell was broken. The doorbell rang that deep musical chime that echoed throughout the entire house. And there was the sound of thudding feet and a yapping bark as Hilary and Caprice galloped down the stairs at top speed to greet our guests.

I could hear Hilary showing them into the little sitting area next to the dining room, a room we rarely used since we normally ate casually at the big kitchen table. Looking around at the chaotic piles of pots and pans around me though, I thought maybe it was for the best if she kept them away from the kitchen altogether.

"There's a platter of finger food already made up in the fridge, Astrid. Maybe you could—" Mr. Ahlberg looked up, taking in for the first time that we were still dressed in our breeches. We'd washed our hands before handling the food of course but there was a smear of dirt across Rob's arm and my shirt had a green slobber mark on it from Red crunching his apple on me. "Er, on second thought, why don't you two clean up. I'll have Linea—"

He broke off again as Hilary's mom came wandering in the back kitchen door from the garden, her hands still muddy with earth and a dreamy far-off look on her face as if she were still thinking about all the things she was about to plant. Her small greenhouse had expanded rapidly and the garden was now her full time job, along with running their bed and breakfast.

"Uh, Linea, we have guests."

"Hmm?" she said absently. "Don't be silly, Rob and Astrid are family, not guests."

"Er, no, in the sitting room. Darius brought his uncle. I texted you. Several times."

"Oh, dear I didn't have my phone on me. Well, Hilary will just have to get them settled while we all clean up. I'm going to shower. Rob, did you bring anything else to wear?"

"No, I didn't think about that."

"No problem. You two stay in what you're in but clean up a little. We won't use the dining room. Set the picnic table out back. It overlooks the water and will keep him distracted. Hopefully. Offer him as much wine as it takes."

Hilary's mom was right. With the table set with selections of delicious one-bite appetizers, copious amounts of wine and a fortunately-timed stunning sunset turning the ocean below us into a riot of colour, Darius's uncle seemed very content.

He'd lived in Canada a long time but had lots of funny stories to tell of his life back in Syria before his country had been bombed to rubble.

The dinner was amazing and conversation flowed easily, ranging from horses, which it turned out Uncle Nabil approved of, to Darius's wins on the Squash court to Hilary's plans for schooling. Spoiler alert: she didn't have any. She'd turned her sights back to being a professional actress but she knew better than to mention it right then.

"So, Astrid," Nabil said turning to me, "Darius tells me that you're becoming an expert at horse archery. My brother's family back in Syria was quite proficient in it."

"Oh, I know," I said enthusiastically, "it was your nephew's videos that inspired me to start in the first place."

"Videos, what videos?" His voice was suddenly sharp and an awkward silence fell over the table.

Darius sent me a warning look but I couldn't exactly stop now.

"Um, well," I cleared my throat. "A long time ago, some of your nephews and, I guess, other cousins made some videos that they put online, on YouTube actually. They were really amazing. They were doing stunt riding and mounted archery. I'd never seen anything like it before. They are—they were—such good riders and the horses looked like they were having so much fun."

I broke off, my cheeks flaming.

Darius's uncle had gone very still and his face had turned an ashy grey, and I wanted to sink into the ground and disappear.

Because of course, even though they were still online, the videos had stopped being made years ago. Right after the war had started and their farm and most of their beautiful horses had been caught by bombing. Some of the young boys riding so effortlessly in the videos had been killed, or kidnapped and forced to fight, or had just never been heard from again. And Darius had said that one of them had been injured so badly that his lower legs had been taken right off. Although he was one of the luckier ones because he could still walk and ride with the help of prosthetics. I knew that part of the ranch was still there though, and that some of the horses had survived.

Darius had hardly been able to talk to me about it when I'd

first met him and it had taken him months before he could watch the videos.

"I'm so sorry," I said, finally finding my voice, "I shouldn't have said anything."

"Darius," Nabil said sharply, "what is this YouTube video thing she's talking about?"

"Just a place to look at videos, Uncle. Yusef was always fooling around making movies, remember? He had a channel and lots of subscribers. They were pretty popular at the time."

"Why didn't I know about any of this?"

"I'm not sure," Darius shrugged. "It never seemed like a big deal at the time. I'd forgotten they'd even existed too until Astrid showed them to me."

"I need to watch these. As soon as we get home you will find them for me. I need to watch them all. We will stay up all night if we have to."

"Of course, Uncle." Darius sighed and shot me an irritated look.

"Well, how about we have some of that beautiful dessert you brought, Darius. Hilary can help you bring it from the kitchen," Hilary's mom said smoothly. "Here, Nabil let me pour you some more wine."

Things got better again after that. Both the Ahlberg's were experts at making people feel at home and soon Nabil was talking and laughing again.

The dessert was delicious. It was something I couldn't properly pronounce called Kaak Bi Loz but the taste was amazing. They were little rectangles made from baked almond marzipan, sugar and other flavours that I couldn't place. They were completely addictive and I had to force myself to eat slowly and not take too many. Nabil had brought dark, fragrant coffee beans that Darius and Hilary ground up and made coffee to go with it. It was so dark and rich I thought it was hands down the best coffee I had ever tasted.

All in all, except for that one incident, it had been a successful dinner and it wasn't until nine o clock that things wrapped up and we were able to slip away in time to meet Rob's dad. Artimax and Ferdi were waiting at the fence for us, ready to go back home to their familiar beds and get a proper dinner.

We led them down the driveway in the dark, their hooves clopping companionably across the packed gravel, one of the best sounds in the world in my opinion.

"Astrid," Rob's dad said, pulling me into an affectionate hug. "Did you manage to cheer this boy up?"

"A little," I said, smiling. Mr. Harris was kind but he wasn't a horse person. He supported Rob a hundred percent but he didn't quite understand what it felt like to have a horse that you loved get sold. Even a horse that wasn't your own left a cold, empty spot inside of you when it left. A hole that couldn't be filled by anything but time.

It was nearly nine thirty by the time I got back to the house, right on the edge of being too late for making a phone call but I decided to risk it. I wanted to hear Aunt Lillian's news and she usually stayed up late working on paperwork anyway.

She picked up on the second ring.

"Astrid!" she bellowed down the line. "Good to hear from you. We need to organize a visit."

I winced and pulled the phone away from my ear. There wasn't any cell service up at the ranch so they relied on the ancient yellow landline attached to her kitchen wall. The reception was usually terrible so she always shouted.

Hearing her voice brought life at the ranch vividly back to me. I could picture her standing in the big kitchen by the stove, probably with a cup of tea in one hand, and her old wolfhound, Jake, lying at her feet.

"Hey, Aunt Lillian. Yes, I'd love to visit. It's been way too long. Rob told me that you want to send him another horse."

"One, two, maybe three. Whatever he'll take, really. I wish I could clone him and send them all to him."

"I think he'd be happy with one or two." I laughed. "Maybe we could fly up for a weekend sometime. Or Rob's dad might even be able to drive us with the horse trailer if we could find a few days that he could get away. I still have to get Antonio to you, too."

"Who?" She bellowed. "Oh, that sheep. Yes, or I could do you one better. How about you come to work for me and I get Allen to pick you, that ridiculous horse and that lamb up and bring you here?"

"Work for you?" I said, ignoring the part where she'd called Red ridiculous. He'd been my late Uncle Trent's horse and had had a few funny quirks when I'd started riding him. Aunt Lillian liked to mock him but I knew she loved him deep down. "Like for the summer?"

"Well, ideally it would be for the whole summer but I know you have a life there. So, I'd say that I'd like you for a month if I can have you."

A whole month. I thought of all my responsibilities here at home and the kids that I taught at the archery range. My coach, Earl, depended on me to help with archery camp and I'd already promised that I would be there. And I helped Oona out at the barn sometimes, too.

"I'm sorry. I just don't think I can get away for that long..."

"Well, I won't say I'm surprised. I know how busy you are there. Your old archery club will be disappointed, though. They've gone a bit mad, to tell you the truth."

"Why, what are they up to?" I asked cautiously.

"They want to hold one of those weird dress-up festivals here. They want to camp in my fields and set up a castle in the upper pasture and everything. It's crazy."

Weird dress up festival? That really didn't sound like the kids I remembered from the archery club at all. Lincoln, Gage, and

Mara had been very unimaginative types of people. I couldn't see them wanting to set up a castle for any reason at all.

"Oh, wait a second," I said, suddenly remembering. "Are you talking about the Society people?"

When I'd lived at the ranch I'd convinced Aunt Lillian to let my school archery club convert one of her old abandoned barns into an indoor range. We'd spent all sorts of time cleaning it out, painting it and setting it up with proper targets.

It turned out that our homemade range was the only place to shoot indoors in the entire area and pretty soon other locals had asked to use the space for archery, too. Gage's older brother Bill had been part of a local society made up of a diverse mixture of gaming and history buffs that liked to dress up like knights and princesses from ancient times and host feasts, mock battles and tournaments.

"That's right, some royal what-not society. Apparently, it's an anniversary year for them or something and they wanted to stage a three-day encampment and some tournaments. Can you picture all those people walking around the ranch wearing silks and armour? And jousting matches? I'm surprised the archery club kids are even suggesting it. That Lincoln seemed like such a nice steady young man, too."

I choked back a laugh. Aunt Lillian was an amazing person but she didn't have much of an imagination, either. It actually sounded like a lot of fun to me. Especially if there were real jousting matches with horses, lances, and armour. I'd pay to see something like that.

"Okay," I said, trying to figure out what any of this had to do with me. "You've lost me. What does a festival have to do with the archery club?"

"Oh, well, I'm sure you wouldn't be interested. It all sounds like a load of hooey to me. It's just that some of those society people from up north who would be coming for the festival also do that mounted archery thing you're always talking about. They wanted to have a little horse archery demonstration and competition during the festival to get new people interested in the sport.

"They had some idea of having a week-long clinic here ahead of the festival and then have a mock tournament just for fun at the end. They even found some teacher who is willing to come all the way from Hungary to teach. Can you imagine that?"

"Wait, what?" I was suddenly all ears.

"Oh, now that caught perked your interest." She laughed. "Laszlo something or other I think his name was. Apparently he teaches all over the world. One of the girls at the club here got all interested and then some other members of the club wanted to try it too."

"Laszlo ... wait, you don't mean Laszlo Belko, do you?"

"Oh, something weird like that, yes. Can you imagine being saddled with a name like that as a child? Although, I suppose it's probably normal if you live in Hungary—"

"Aunt Lillian," I broke in. "He's actually really famous. He competes all over the world. And he only does a handful of clinics every year. Are you certain he'd come all this way to teach?"

"That's what they told me. Apparently he's friends with some people in this part of Canada and he likes to visit. As long as they have enough people signed up for the clinic then he'll come. I told those Society people no of course, because all this talk of castles and tournaments sounded crazy, but then I thought it was something you might like to try."

"Yes," I said quickly, "definitely. It would be an amazing opportunity."

"Well, that's a different story then," Aunt Lillian said in a suddenly business-like voice, "the clinic itself would be a week-long event with that weird festival at the end of it but, if you're serious, then I'd like you to come up ahead of time to help get some of the horses ready."

Before I could ask any questions she moved along and I had to listen hard to keep up.

"Not all the people who want to sign up for the clinic have their own horses, or can afford to bring them this far, and I'd like to lease them some of ours. We have all those trail horses not being used. They're as bombproof as they come. Or at least, they were. They haven't been used in a while. They'd need to be desensitized to the bows and arrows and whatever else you'd need to teach them ahead of time. And then during the clinic and the, er, festival, I'd need help making sure everything was organized and that the guests were fed and taken care of. You do all that and I'll sponsor your entry fee. You could bring Rob along too, of course. That gives him time to pick out some horses to take back with him."

"Oh, wow, Aunt Lillian, that sounds amazing," I said, finally getting a word in edgewise.

"I was hoping you'd feel that way. We miss you around here, Astrid. You've been away too long."

I winced, feeling a stab of guilt. Life was just so busy all the time. I barely had enough time to breathe let alone think about going on vacation. This past winter I'd been focused on archery and helping out at the range. The few spare minutes that I'd managed to scrape together I spent with Red and Rob.

"I really hope I can come," I said, "but I have to check with my coach, Earl, first. I already promised to help with archery camp this summer. And I was supposed to help out with the bed and breakfast here once school is done. The restaurant will be opening for breakfast this summer, too. So I'm just not sure if they'll need me for that."

I broke off, my mind working overtime to try and imagine a way that I could go. Suddenly that's all I wanted to do. Riding with Laszlo Belko would be the chance of a lifetime. Plus I could see all my friends, both human and animal, at the ranch again.

"Well, that's up to you to organize," Aunt Lillian said in her brusque voice. "I really hope you can figure it all out. Like I said, we'd love to have you here. You call me in a couple of days and let me know one way or another."

Later, I lay in bed that night unable to sleep at all. My mind was whirling and I was practically shaking with excitement. It had been too late to text Rob by the time I was off the phone but I would send him a message first thing in the morning. I'd already sent Earl an email to see what he thought and tomorrow I'd talk to Hilary and her parents to find out if they could do without me for an entire month.

Even though the farm was better staffed now since the Ahlbergs had hired the elderly Alfred and his wife Hanna to help out, there was always plenty of work to do. Between school and riding, I helped with the barn chores and the farm animals and the bed and breakfast. Summer was a busy time. There was a chance they wouldn't be able to let me go at all.

I finally fell into a restless sleep, dreaming of galloping through a wide grassy field at sunset surrounded by a forest of towering pines. But far off in the darkening trees an owl called, it's cry drawn out and mournful. Even in my sleep, I shivered.

CHAPTER 3

Two days later it was all sorted. It had been almost *too* easy and to be honest, I'd been a little offended when things fell into place so seamlessly. Apparently I wasn't as indispensable as I'd thought.

"Of course you can go, honey," Hilary's mom had said at breakfast when I'd haltingly brought up the idea of me leaving for a month. "We have Hanna to help with the bed and breakfast, and Hilary will pitch in too, won't you dear?"

"Yeah, yeah," Hilary had said, around a mouthful of cereal. "Seriously, go, Astrid. This place will be fine. Horse archery is your destiny. Don't deny your destiny."

She grinned at me when I rolled my eyes.

"Anyway, you should be happy to be getting away for a while. You're going to see Liza and Justin again, not to mention Folly and Quarry. And you get to spend a whole, basically unsupervised, month with your boyfriend. Besides, you need something good to take your mind off, you know, *things.*"

Right, the baby. We didn't really talk about her very much except when Marion called to give Mrs. Ahlberg updates. I still wasn't really talking to my stepmom although we did email back and forth sometimes. The hurt and fear from that night I'd run away still clung to me after all this time and I still didn't want to have much to do with either of them. Even them living all the way in Alaska felt too close sometimes.

"But I'm abandoning you and Oona with all the barn work," I said, changing the subject quickly. "And I'd be leaving you with Caprice to take care of. I won't be here to help with the bed and breakfast or the restaurant. And I'll miss Ellie's first show in her new home."

I was grasping at straws by then but Ellie *had* been my project horse and her new family had specifically invited me to watch her compete.

"Ellie has a whole lifetime of showing ahead of her," Hilary said in a bored voice. "Caprice loves it here, Oona is too self-absorbed to miss you, and we have *staff* to do the barn work." She glanced up quickly at her mother with one eyebrow arched to show she was teasing. Mostly.

"What Hilary is *trying* to say," her mother said, giving her daughter a meaningful look. "Is that you deserve a vacation. You work hard here and this will be a nice treat for you."

"Thank you." I said "I'd only go if you were really sure it was okay."

"It's more than okay. I think you should pack your bags. This will be exciting."

"I don't even want to think about packing yet. I have no idea what to take. At least Red and the sheep are easy to pack for."

Hilary made a disapproving choking noise on her cereal and fixed me with a glare. "Please tell me that you are not going to pack *outfits* for those sheep."

She sounded so offended that I burst into laughter.

"No, I swear, not a single one. Aunt Lillian would think I was completely nuts if I dressed up a farm animal."

"Good, she's right. I hope I never have to see Callie's stupid sheep fashion page again."

"Oh come on, admit it. You secretly loved it."

Our youngest boarder, Callie, had created an online fan page for the barn, filling it with hundreds of photos of her cheeky Welsh pony, Mister Sox and the other animals, and sometimes people, who lived at the farm. She was forever creeping around taking pictures and more than once I'd been surprised, and horrified, to find grubby, dirt-smeared, images of myself cleaning stalls or scrubbing water buckets when they were posted online. The most popular one had been of me, sitting on a hay bale, sharing bits of my sandwich with Portia who happened to be wearing a plaid dog jacket at the time.

Callie's photos didn't exactly fit in with the elegant image that Hilary wanted our farm to project but they'd gained us a ton of followers. The photo of me and Portia had somehow been seen, and commented on, by a few upper level riders which had led to Callie devoting weeks of photos just to the sheep. Which had irritated Hilary to no end.

That photo had even been featured in the online magazine, SheepLife, which had annoyed her even more.

One of my favourite boarders, Pender, had given the two of them their beautiful matching red collars with their names printed on little brass tags. Then Sadie had thought that they might be cold in the middle of winter so she'd bought them the matching plaid dog jackets that looked like miniature horse coats. And then when Easter rolled around, Callie had appeared with rabbit ears for both of them so she could take photos and then that started a flurry of outfits and hats. Then the famous sandwich photo had taken off, which made Callie completely devote the farm page to sheep couture.

"Just make sure to take *both* those stupid sheep with you when you go. I don't want to be stuck babysitting Portia while you're gone."

"Umm, I'm not sure if Aunt Lillian..."

"Nope, that's the deal," Hilary said firmly, "if you go, the mutton goes, too."

Earl's phone call came later in the day. "I got your email, Astrid. This Laszlo guy looks like a big deal. I think you should go for it. Nicole, the girl who helps me teach on Saturdays, would like to go away for the last part of August. She's already said that she'll take your days if you take hers."

I was off the hook for barn chores, too.

"Oh, go have a good time," Oona had said, raising her eyebrows. "Marcy asked if she could work off some lessons on Oreo so that's good timing. You can spend the next few weeks training her up to do your job."

As nice as it was to have things happen so smoothly, it was a little insulting to discover how easily replaceable I was in pretty much all areas of my life.

"You're overthinking this," Rob told me when I'd poured everything out to him on the phone that night. "Everyone just wants you to have a good time."

"I'm not sure how much of a good time I'll have if you don't get to come."

"Oh, I'm sure you'd forget all about me by the second week." He laughed. "And my dad didn't say a definite no; just that he'd have to think about it. He really wanted me to help him full-time at the office this summer." He paused and sighed. "But my cousin already said that he'd be interested in doing an internship with Dad if I wasn't going to be around. So, we'll see."

"Oh," I said, feeling an extra spark of excitement. This trip would be so much more fun if Rob could come along. I couldn't imagine being away from him for a whole month. And it wasn't like we could text everyday either when I was up there with the terrible cell and internet service at the ranch.

"I don't have any shows lined up for Artimax yet," he went on, "and the entries haven't been posted for Ferdi's season. Honestly, he could probably have a month off anyway. He's been working pretty hard all winter and I don't want to overwhelm his small pea-brain."

I had to agree with that one. Ferdi was sweet and kind and a flashy mover, but he was perhaps not the brightest of lights. It was like his body had grown and developed, but his mind stayed that of a two-year-old baby horse.

"So, what you're saying is you might be able to come after all."

"Maybe, but don't get your hopes up," he said firmly. "Worst case scenario is that I could come up for a few days near the end of your trip to visit everyone and pick out those new projects. But don't let it change your plans, Astrid. You need to do this."

"Yeah, no. I'm totally going. But I really would miss you."

CHAPTER 4

That night, Aunt Lillian nearly blew my eardrum off with her enthusiastic whoop when I told her that Red, the sheep, and I would be coming to visit.

"Oh, this is perfect. We're going to have so much fun. I won't deny that there will be a lot of work to do too, but we'll do our best to keep you entertained. There have been a few changes around here that I think you'll approve of. I didn't think the dressage thing was going to fly in this neighbourhood, but apparently Liza has worked some sort of miracle and it has caught on. Our lesson program is booming. We could always use more help up here permanently too, Astrid. If you need a change of scenery, you're always welcome to stay here full time."

"Thanks, Aunt Lillian," I said laughing. She offered to have me move there pretty much every time I talked to her. Even the Christmas card she'd sent in the mail had had a little note about it at the bottom. But the truth was that, for now at least, the Ahlberg's farm felt like home. I'd been a little lost after they'd taken me in, but now I felt settled and it was a good place to put down roots and grow a little.

And two days later, Rob called me with the good news. He

had been given the all-clear to go and he was allowed to enter the week-long clinic too. I was so excited that I probably squealed as loud as Aunt Lillian had.

This summer was shaping up to be one of the most exciting ones yet.

It turned out that there was one small, very feisty person I'd forgotten to tell.

Our boarder, Annie, had two daughters: pint-sized Callie who was always into everything, and her moody older sister Nori.

Although she'd been awful in the beginning, Nori and I had become good friends over the last year. She was leasing Rob's other project horse Maverick and she took regular archery lessons with Earl at the range. We rode on the trails together nearly every weekend, and when she'd started her first year at Sacred Heart, the school that Rob and I both went to, I'd tried to keep an eye on her to make sure she was fitting in.

At first, everything had seemed fine, but the last few months she'd become withdrawn and angry again. The only time she seemed happy lately was at the range and when she was riding Maverick.

Lately, she'd been spending less time at the barn than usual, which was very out of character for her. And it also meant that she'd missed the memo when I'd told everyone else at the barn that I was going to visit the ranch.

So it was quite a surprise one evening to look up and find her standing in the tack room doorway with her hands on her hips, staring at both me and Hilary with a blazing expression on her face. For such a tiny person she sure packed a lot of fury.

"So, when were you planning to tell me that you're going away to a fantastic horse archery camp without me? And for a whole month, too. Nice way to abandon your friends, Astrid."

She sent a pointed glare toward Hilary, who she'd never quite gotten along with anyway.

"Don't look at *me*," Hilary said, raising her tack sponge in the air in surrender. "I'm certainly not going."

We'd been sitting in the big tack room in the main barn cleaning bridles together. Most of the boarders were good about cleaning their own stuff, but there were certain riders who just forgot their bridles on the cleaning hook for weeks if you didn't remind them. Sometimes it was just easier to do it ourselves.

"Oh, hey Nori," I said, gulping a little as I took in her furious expression. "I didn't see you there."

"No, obviously not, since you were busy making secret plans without me."

"Nothing is a secret." I said patiently, sighing inwardly. She was a good person but she had quite the temper. She had the habit of leaping into an irrational storm of anger one minute and then being all sunshine an hour later. It was very disconcerting "Things just sort of happened last minute. I didn't even really know if I could go away myself until a couple of days ago."

"And you didn't even think to ask me to go along even though horse archery is the one, single thing that I love to do." It was a statement, not a question.

"Um, I didn't think…"

"No, I guess you didn't care to invite me. But of course perfect Rob is going."

"Yes, he is," I said, struggling to keep my own temper in check. Really, what business of hers was it where Rob and I went? I really wasn't obligated to have her tag along everywhere. But there was something in the way she held her head and the way her jaw trembled that told me she was really more hurt than angry. "He's helping get the horses ready for the clinic. And then he's picking up some new projects to bring home."

"I could help get the horses ready, too," she said quickly.

"Astrid, you can't go away for practically the whole summer. I'd have nobody to ride with. I'll be all alone."

Her voice cracked suddenly and she took a sharp, gasping breath and quickly looked away.

I stared at her in astonishment, wondering what on earth was going on. She was always dramatic but now she seemed to be genuinely upset. We hadn't even spent that much time together lately so I wasn't sure exactly what was going through her head.

"I know you're a great rider, Nori, but we'd be away for a whole month. Your mom would never let you..."

"Sure she would," Nori interrupted. "She would love to get rid of me for a month. And I need to get away. I need—" Suddenly her phone pinged sharply, first once, and then again and again in rapid fire succession.

"Whoa, I guess you have a few messages," Hilary said, raising her eyebrows.

"Yep." Without even looking at the screen Nori pulled her phone out of her pocket and punched a few buttons until the thing shut up.

Then she took a deep breath, wiping a hand impatiently across her eyes.

"Nori, what is going on? Did something happen at school or ..." I paused, my heart sinking. "Or did something happen between you and your, er, Jackson?"

Nori was only fourteen, but she'd recently started almost-dating the world's worst non-boyfriend. I guess he was good-looking in a dark, sulky sort of way. But he was moody, he had a temper, and he was usually only pleasant when things were going his way. Nori had also told me that he didn't believe in traditional relationships because he didn't like being tied down to any one person so they weren't officially going out. But he also didn't want *her* seeing anyone else.

I didn't know him well since we didn't move in the same circles, but from what I'd seen and the rumours I'd heard, I didn't like him at all. I had been horrified when she'd started hanging out with him but she, in typical Nori style, had refused to listen.

"You just don't understand him," she'd told me. "People don't realize how sensitive and artistic he is. He's a really beautiful person, Astrid."

I could definitely *not* agree with that last part but she was right about the art thing. He was a bit of a genius when it came to art class and there were a few of his paintings hanging in the hallway near the office. If he'd been a halfway decent human being, I would have loved to have introduced him to Oona. As it was, I'd secretly talked to Nori's mom, Annie, about him, but it wasn't like she could refuse to let them hang out at school or anything.

Lately, I'd been so caught up in organizing my own life and worrying about Marion's baby that I hadn't been spending much time with Nori at all, and I probably hadn't been keeping as close an eye on her as I should have been.

"Nori, seriously, what's going on?"

"Nothing," she said, her lower lip suddenly trembling. "As if you care anyway. I guess we're not even real friends or you would have invited me to go with you. You're just like everyone else."

"Of course we're friends…" I started but she'd already turned on her heel and stormed out again, slamming the tack room door behind her. Twice.

"Wow, I hope *we* weren't that dramatic at fourteen," Hilary said, rolling her eyes. "She should seriously consider doing some amateur theater this summer if she's looking for something to do. She can turn on those tears at the drop of a hat."

"I don't think she's faking it," I said with a sigh. "Nori feels everything hard. I hate that Jackson kid, though. She could do so much better. I'd better not find out he's done anything to her."

"Well, it sounds like him breaking up with her wouldn't be such a bad thing."

"Yeah, except I heard he has a habit of punishing people who he decides he doesn't like anymore. Good thing summer is coming and she can take a break from him for a while. Maybe you could keep an eye on her while I'm gone."

"Oh, heck no. She's your pet, not mine. I can't imagine you dragging her up to the ranch, though. She'd be a nightmare."

"She's not that bad, really. The kids at archery class love her. Earl was talking about having her help with some camps this summer. I'd better talk to Annie and see what's going on."

I waited until Nori was safely out on the trails with Maverick before I found her mom practicing in the outdoor ring. Annie's horse, Norman, was trotting around happily, his ears flopping as he obediently leg-yielded down the long side and then did a ten metre circle in the corner before doing a few steps of shoulder-in down the short side.

"Oh, hey Astrid," Annie called, bringing the big warmblood down to a walk and giving him an enthusiastic pat on the neck. "How perfect does this boy look to you?"

"Fantastic. And happy."

"He's always a happy guy but his lessons with Oona agree with him. I'm excited to try some shows with him this season. But you've probably come to talk to me about Nori, right?"

"Yeah, she seemed really upset when she found out I was going away. I wanted to ask you if you knew what was going on with her."

"Ah, well," Annie gave Norman another pat, nosed her feet free of the stirrups, and swung her legs gently back and forth to stretch them out. "She honestly doesn't tell me much of anything, Astrid. She's always been very stubborn and independent. Over the years I've learned to sort of wait for her to confide in me. If I push her then she'll just withdraw completely. I'm sure it has to do with Jackson, though. They had a fight on the phone last week. Nori was very upset afterward."

"That figures," I said darkly. "Do you know what it was about?"

"She won't tell me." Annie made a face. "But I know something happened at school as well. She did tell me that he didn't hurt her, at least physically anyway. Unfortunately, that's all I know. I was hoping she'd confide in you."

"We haven't spent as much time together lately. She told me she wants to come with us to the ranch for a month, though."

"Oh, would you take her with you, Astrid?" Annie looked at me hopefully. "I would pay for her clinic of course, and for her room and board, and something extra for you to keep an eye on her. Whatever you need. I think she could really use some time away."

Well, now I've done it, I thought ruefully, *there's no turning back now.*

"You don't have to pay me to look after her," I said quickly. It wasn't that I didn't need the money, but it didn't feel quite right to take it. And I knew Nori would be furious if she found out that I'd been paid just to hang out with her and be her friend. "But I'll ask Aunt Lillian when I call her tonight. I think she could use some extra help around the farm too, so maybe if Nori pitched in that would cover the room and board and you'd just have to pay for the clinic. I'll check with her anyway."

"Astrid, you are a miracle-worker. I think this would be just what she needs right now. Thank you so much. I owe you big time."

"No you don't," I said, flushing. Annie had already done a lot for me. She'd driven me many times to the range even when Nori wasn't scheduled to be there. She also owned a chain of fitness centers on the Island and had gotten me and Rob free gym memberships for Christmas and set us up with personal trainers and everything. We didn't have a ton of extra time but we made sure to go at least once a week for cardio and strength training. It had nearly killed me in the beginning, but gradually I'd learned to love it. Especially when my archery scores started to improve and I could feel my core activating automatically during my rides.

That night Aunt Lillian was enthusiastic when I told her about Rob and Nori wanting to come.

"Oh, yes, the more the merrier, Astrid. There is a lot of work to do and I want you to be happy here so bring whoever you like. I'll e-mail you the registration forms and waivers for the clinic tomorrow morning. You all need to sign them and get them back to me to reserve your spots. Payment is by credit card. Except for you, of course."

"Thanks again," I said, "you really don't have to pay for me." Although, in reality, I didn't actually have any money to pay for the clinic on my own.

"Oh, it's the least I can do," she said brusquely. "I'll let you know as soon as I've organized your transportation."

I waited until the next day to approach Nori with my plan.

I'd already printed off her paperwork and had it ready in my hand when I caught up with her brushing Maverick in his stall. She didn't see me at first and I took a second to take in how sad and withdrawn she looked. There were dark circles around her eyes and her cheeks were blotchy as if she'd been recently crying.

"Hey, Nori," I said softly, not wanting to startle her.

She jerked a little and Maverick threw up his head and flattened his ears at me, which was his typical expression when he was dealing with anyone but Nori. He was the crankiest horse in existence and he only cared about one person besides himself.

"Hello," she said stiffly, not looking at me.

"Look, I asked my aunt last night if there was still space in the archery clinic for you. She said there's room for you if you like, and that you could come to the ranch and stay with us there."

Nori's brush stilled against Maverick's coat for a second and then continued on again as if she hadn't heard me.

"That's nice," she said finally. "No thanks."

"Come on, Nori," I said, already prepared for this reaction. "You know you'll love it. And Aunt Lillian really needs our help to get the horses ready. You're a good rider and a good archer. If you help us out for the month that will cover your room and board. Your mom will just have to pay for the clinic. You could bring Maverick, too."

"Really?" She couldn't help the interested expression that flickered across her face. "Are you sure I won't be getting in your way? I don't want to be some third wheel on your and Rob's vacation. I don't want you to think you'd have to babysit me the whole time or anything. I just need … I need to get out of here for a while."

"No, of course you won't be in the way," I said quickly. "There will be lots to do there. And there are miles of trails to explore, too. You can try riding Maverick western if you like."

"You mean with a cowboy hat and boots?" she said distastefully. "No thank you."

"Don't knock it until you try it."

"Don't try and change me, Astrid," Nori said dramatically. "I'm a wild spirit that can't be contained."

She shot me a grin to show that she was at least partially kidding.

"Here's your paperwork," I said, praying that I was not making a mistake by planning to spend a whole month with this moody weirdo.

"Thanks, Astrid. I mean it. Seriously, you won't regret this."

"You are totally going to regret that," Hilary said later that night. She laughed and took another spoonful of ice cream from the tub we were finishing off together. It was nearly eleven and I had school the next day, but I couldn't sleep with all the exciting things that were happening lately. "She is such a brat."

"Oh, she's all right. Just stubborn and dramatic. She'll probably grow up to be a lawyer or a politician or something."

"Yeah, or a criminal."

We grinned at each other.

"Seriously though, I am going to miss you, Astrid. Make sure Lillian doesn't convince you to stay there forever. I need you back."

"Of course I'll be back. Otherwise, you're going to make my dog gain twenty pounds in ice cream alone."

Caprice sat on Hilary's lap with her chin resting on the table. The lid to the ice cream tub sat in front of her like a little plate and every so often Hilary would drop a chunk of vanilla there for her to work on.

"What? She likes it," Hilary said, patting the little dog's head. "Don't listen to her, Caprice, I'm going to be a great babysitter. You just wait and see."

CHAPTER 5

After that, things began to move at breakneck speed. I still had archery practice, lessons and a couple of local tournaments to shoot at. At every tournament, I did my own rounds and then hurried to help the younger kids get ready for theirs. I hated to admit it but I'd been shooting for so many years now that the lustre of competing had worn off a little. I had competed at these local venues dozens, if not hundreds, of times. It was old news for me. But to see the excitement of the little kids who were maybe competing for their first time brought back a lot of old memories. Some of the best years of my life had been spent doing this. So why didn't it complete me the way it had in the past?

The weeks flew by and, before I knew it, my exams were written and my school year was finally behind me. The summer holidays had officially started.

Our departure time was on us and suddenly, I felt like I had a million loose ends to wrap up and only a short time to do it in. And that's when the panic set in again.

"You're absolutely, one hundred percent sure this is really

okay?" I asked for the millionth time, looking down anxiously at the open suitcase on my bed. Despite my best efforts, it was only half-packed and the rest of my clothes sat in unorganized heaps on both the bed and the floor. I had exactly one day left to pack and right now it seemed impossible. Red's stuff was all organized, of course, but then he didn't need a different outfit for every single day of the week like I did.

"Yes, stop worrying." Hillary didn't look up from her dressage magazine. She'd sprawled herself across the top half of my bed, one of my pillows hugged to her chest and Caprice curled up next to her elbow. Hilary was supposed to be there for moral support but she'd quickly gotten distracted by an article on custom boots.

"I think I really need a pair of these," she said dreamily, tracing her index finger across the toe of a burgundy crocodile-print boot. She sighed and glanced up at me. "Look, Astrid. Everything is running on its own just fine here. Personally, I'm looking forward to an entire month without a single sheep in the barn."

"Yeah, yeah, you know you'll miss them." I threw another pair of socks into my suitcase and stared down at the pile of clothes, frowning. Why on earth was packing so hard?

"I don't know why they have so many ads in these things now," Hilary said, flipping another page of her magazine. "There are barely any articles. If I were ever running a magazine, I'd do things completely differently. Maybe that's what I should do in my spare time, start my own magazine."

"Hmm," I said, half-listening. I held up two pairs of schooling breeches, trying to decide between them, then finally threw them both in the suitcase.

"Astrid," Hilary sat up finally and looked at me with a no-nonsense expression, "you're going to be fine. There are whole team of people here to look after this farm so you don't have to worry about anything."

"But, Caprice ..."

"... will be perfectly okay with us. We love her and she sleeps with my parents half the time anyway. Don't worry, we'll spoil her rotten."

I knew it was true. Sometime in the middle of the winter, Caprice had started dividing her loyalties between me and the Ahlbergs. I guessed it was because she was home with them all day while I was at school. It was nice that she was loved but I still felt a little jealous. And a little anxious about leaving her behind.

"I still wish Aunt Lillian would have let me bring her," I said. Aunt Lillian's only stipulation to our visit had been that I leave Caprice at home since her big wolfhound Jake was getting old and cranky. He didn't really like other dogs much, although he loved people.

"Less chit-chat, more packing," Hilary said, rolling to her feet. "Actually, wait, don't you have a lesson to get to? You go, I'll pack."

"But ..."

"Go, you can always reorganize everything when you get back. At least I'll have gotten you off to a proper start. Honestly, it's like you've never packed a suitcase before in your life."

"Right, okay, thank you." She would do a much better job at packing than I would anyway. I looked over at the clock and headed for the door reluctantly. I had so much to do; I must have been crazy to think I could squeeze in a last minute lesson the day before I left.

Still, the moment I hit the barn all my doubts and worries just sort of melted away. Red and Portia were eating their breakfast side by side with their noses close together. Antonio was curled up in a pile of hay beside them, his eyes half-closed and his chin resting on one outstretched foreleg.

It was such a peaceful scene and I was suddenly hit with the feeling of how truly lucky I was to even be there. Three years ago I would never have even dreamt of having a horse of my own, or any pet at all actually. Or dreamt of a life where my father's all-consuming presence wasn't hanging over me like a dagger waiting to fall.

It had been a long, hard journey and I barely recognized the scared, lonely girl I'd been at the time.

Red looked up and whickered softly under his breath when he caught sight of me, his ears pricked as he came forward to gently search my pockets.

"Hey, buddy," I whispered, straightening his forelock, "are you looking extra-cute because you know I have treats?"

He gave my pocket a tug and I laughingly pushed him away and fished out the carrot chunks I'd brought for him. I gave Portia her share, too.

Antonio scrambled to his feet as soon as he heard the sound of crunching food, shook the shavings free from his coat, and trotted over to me, rearing up and putting his little hooves on the wall so he could get closer to me.

"You're getting pretty pushy there, friend," I told him, tickling the end of his nose and giving him a tiny piece of carrot. "I don't think they're going to let you get away with that sort of stuff at the ranch."

Red was already pretty clean but I polished his coat with a soft brush, picked out his feet and smoothed out his silky mane and tail. I tacked him up quickly, tossed the sheep some grain for a distraction, and then headed across the paddock and up the pathway to the indoor.

It was dark and silent when I went in, the air noticeably cooler than the warm, spring sunshine outside. I felt a pulse of excitement. No matter how many times I rode in there, it always felt like I was entering some sort of sacred space. The rich smell of the footing, the stillness, the light filtering softly in from the skylights. It felt like the whole place held its breath, waiting for Red and me to create something magical.

I slipped on his back and let my legs dangle at his sides, my hips swaying slightly with his long, rhythmic strides.

"Good morning," Oona called from across the ring, sliding the rolling door shut behind her.

She had the required travel mug of coffee in her hands and was watching us with her head tilted slightly to one side.

I didn't mind her scrutiny like I had when she'd first arrived at the farm. She was exacting and bossy and could see the tiniest mistakes, but she was also kind and I'd learned to both like and trust her; she'd never do anything to hurt the horses.

This was actually one of the first under saddle lessons I'd had with her in a long time. We usually just worked Red on the ground in the long-lines.

"Looking good," she said as I moved Red up into a trot, "fix that right ankle, slightly more flexion to the left. Honestly, Liza is going to freak out when she sees how well this horse is going."

I smiled, guiding Red in a series of gentle looping serpentines across the arena, silently agreeing with her. I circled at the top of the ring, spiraling my track inward and then outward again, capturing his shoulder just as it began to drift.

"Good," Oona said.

We concentrated on our trot work until Red was completely loose and supple, then I gave the signal and he sprang eagerly into a canter as if he'd been waiting for the opportunity.

When I'd first gotten Red, it was like he'd been allergic to going forward at all and now he loved it. He'd canter all day long if given the chance. I did the serpentines again, carefully asking for a lead change right before we switched directions. He leapt into them enthusiastically, giving a happy skip each time. He felt like he was showing off.

"I think you'd better tell your aunt you'd like to buy that horse," Oona said a half hour later, once I'd brought Red down to a walk and was cooling him out on a long rein.

"What?" I said, coming out of my haze of euphoria. I was glad

I'd made time for a lesson after all. Riding a horse always had a way of putting things in perspective for me. Suddenly, my trip to the ranch didn't seem so overwhelming anymore. I was going to get to have a vacation and ride for a whole month. What could be better?

Oona's words hit me from left-field.

"Well, I know he's supposed to be a permanent lease but once your aunt sees how well he's going she might change her mind. He looks like a different horse now. He's worth a lot more money than before too."

"She would never do that," I said, but I could hear an uncertain note in my voice. "He was my Uncle Trent's horse."

"Right, of course. I just know what it's like to put a lot of work and ..." she paused, "a lot of love, into a horse only to have them taken away at the last minute. It is not something I would wish for you."

She got a far-off look on her face, and I knew she was thinking about that other place and time, halfway across the world, where she used to teach. I think of the painting on her wall of the beautiful white horse piaffing in a dark arena. I knew his name, Furioso, but other than that she never talked about him.

I reached down and rubbed Red's damp neck.

"Thank you," I said finally, "but that won't happen with Red. My aunt made a promise to my uncle that she would never sell him and she made that same promise to me. I'd trust her with my life."

"Okay." Oona sighed. "I just thought I'd mention it. Horse people are unpredictable when there is money on the table. Not many of them can resist a good offer. Will you come up for a tea after you're done cooling him out? I have something for you to take to Liza for me."

"Sure," I said, "of course. I'm just going to give this guy a bath."

I tried to shake off Oona's words as I ran the lukewarm water over Red's back. She and I had become friends over the last year, but she was still a little strange sometimes. I knew that she'd had some sort of trauma happen back in Belgium where she'd been teaching. The rumour was that it had involved a bad break-up of some sort, but I'd never been brave enough to ask. She was a very private person, and also slightly scary, so I just kept my questions to myself and hoped that she'd share on her own eventually.

"She's right about one thing though, Red, you are looking mighty handsome if I do say so myself."

Instead of taking him back to his paddock, I used his bridle to lead him down the driveway to the big pastures below and turned him out into the grassy field on the right where his buddy Oreo was spending the day.

His coat was still slightly damp, so as soon as he ambled into the grassy field, he dropped down to his knees and then flopped over onto one side to have a good roll. He waved his feet in the air as he itched his back and neck and then, with a grunt and a groan, he popped back upright and trotted off to join his friends.

"Have fun. Make good choices," I called, although in Red's case it wasn't really necessary. He wasn't like Rabbit, or Hilary's horse Jerry, who would sometimes blaze around the field so fast they looked like they'd fall and break their legs at any second. He was always steady, dependable, and wise.

Oona already had the kettle boiling and a lemon cake on the table by the time I made it upstairs to her loft above the barn.

It was a cozy, sunny apartment stuffed with books and art with a small balcony overlooking the pastures. Basically my dream house.

As always, I went straight to the stack of paintings against the far wall to look at her newest projects.

Oona was a talented artist whose paintings sold all over the world. Right now her three easels were full of the same horse in different poses.

She had captured the arrogant eye, the tossing mane and the

belligerent buck perfectly; the paintings were of her own horse, Pants, who she had adopted last season. He was turning out to be a project and a half, although he was just as beautiful in real life as he was in the paintings.

"Nice," I said, gazing at the third one, which caught him in full prance; you could just see how full of himself he was. "Where's the Horses in Myth series? You can't be done already."

"Yep, they shipped off last week. The paintings of Pants are for that fundraiser at the end of the month for the racehorse adoption place. They wanted a progress video of how he was coming along but I thought I'd just donate the paintings instead."

"Good idea." I laughed. Pants was much better behaved than when he'd first arrived, but that wasn't saying very much. He had the busiest mind of any horse I'd ever met and he spent every spare second you were with him trying to cause trouble of some sort. Every. Second.

Even getting him in from his paddock and tacking him up was a marathon. He was just so mouthy; he'd latch his teeth on whatever came near him: lead ropes, jackets, skin, fancy saddles, anything. And when he wasn't biting, he was kicking, pawing, or trying to squash you against the wall. And he didn't act like he was angry when he was doing it; he seemed to genuinely be having a great time. His ears would be pricked and his eyes gleaming with maniacal fun, his little upper lip twitching whenever he was about to do something awful.

I didn't even turn him out to pasture on my own; I left that for Oona to deal with since he was likely to just grab the lead rope in his mouth and bolt for fun, dragging his handler down the driveway behind him.

But, from a distance, he was stunning. He moved like a top-level horse, his bay coat glistened and his silky mane and tail never had a hair out of place. The arrogance that made him such a pain to deal with also gave grace and power to his movements, even when he was just walking around his paddock. He didn't stroll or lounge like the other horses did; he moved with the panther-like grace of a predator and he was always alert and watching.

"He's coming along," Oona said, "you watch, by the time you get back from the ranch he'll be a different horse."

"I hope so," I muttered under my breath, too softly for her to hear.

We drank our tea and ate cake while the sunshine streamed in and made patterns on the wall. We talked about horses and painting, and I confessed again how worried I was about leaving the farm for so long.

"It will be fine," she said flatly, "you'll get over it."

Oona wasn't exactly one to offer sympathy. She was more of a get on with it and stop whining type of person.

"I know, but I can't help feeling the way I do."

"Maybe not, but you can stop dwelling on the worrisome things and focus on something else. That's your choice."

"Hmm."

"Anyway, I didn't bring you up here just to stuff you with cake. I have a present for Liza and actually one for you too, but you can't have yours until you get back."

"Hey, that's not fair."

"Nope, but it means you can't run away to that ranch forever if there's a painting waiting for you here."

"Ah, tricky. Okay. Is mine of Red? Or is it of Portia? If it's a sheep then I'm definitely hanging it in the living room. Hilary will love that."

"Maybe, I'm not telling you." A smile tugged at the corner of her mouth. "I'm sending Liza's with you so you have to take care of it. It will be in a case but you can't squash it or anything. And bring the case back with you too, they're not cheap."

"Okay, yes, I promise."

She got up and went to the bookshelf, picking up two slim

packages that were propped up against it. One was larger and the other was half the size. They were wrapped in plain brown paper.

"Yours is the smaller one. And I'll set it right here on this shelf for when you get back."

"Hey, that's mean."

"Yes, and here is Liza's. You should be there when she opens it, though. I think you'll like it."

She laid the painting into a thin, black case that was lined with foam and clicked it shut.

"I won't see you off tomorrow morning so I'll say my goodbyes now. Everything will be fine here. You make sure you stay strong and take care of yourself. Don't let anyone else make decisions for you. And come back safely. Goodbye."

She'd been shepherding me toward the door while she talked and as soon as I was near the landing she pushed the case with the painting into my arms, shooed me outside and then abruptly shut the door behind me.

It was such an Oona-like move that I couldn't help but laugh. She was the absolute worst with anything involving emotions.

Holding the case carefully, I went slowly downstairs, my thoughts drifting back to the other painting, the one that was mine, waiting for me.

CHAPTER 6

The trailer crunched up the driveway at exactly 4:30 am, which was when we needed to start loading up if we were to catch the early morning ferry to the mainland.

Rob, Artimax, and Ferdi had already been dropped off the night before. Artimax was making the long trip with us of course, and Ferdi was staying at the farm so he could have his own vacation. He was going to have a few weeks off, and then Oona was going to do some gentle work with him on the long-lines.

Rob had his own farm but with Possum sold and Artimax away, Ferdi would have been all alone so it was nicer for him to be at Home Farm with the other horses.

Nori had been dropped off about an hour ago, pale-faced and half-asleep, and she'd made herself busy getting Maverick ready for his big trailer ride and doing her best to ignore her mother who was fluttering around trying to help.

"Allan," I called in delight as soon as the huge trailer pulled to a stop. Allan was an old friend of my aunts and had driven me to and from the ranch a few times in the past. It was a long trip and we'd spent lots of time talking about all sorts of things so had grown to be friends.

"Looking good, Astrid," he said, accepting the coffee I held out to him with one hand and giving me a one-armed hug with the other. The first time he'd driven me anywhere had been just after my terrible accident with Folly when I'd been bruised and bandaged in all sorts of ways. I think he half-expected me to be injured every time he saw me now and was pleasantly surprised to find me in one piece.

He shook Rob's hand and nodded pleasantly to Nori who had appeared in the barn doorway, white-faced and clutching Maverick's lead rope as if it were a lifeline. She looked like she hadn't slept all night. Her phone rang suddenly, unnaturally loud in the early morning hours and she fished around until she found it and shut it off.

"Who on earth would be calling you at this time in the morning?" Annie asked, looking concerned.

"It's nothing. Just a wrong number," Nori said briskly, "probably a telemarketer."

Her mother raised her eyebrows and silently looked away with a sigh and a shake of her head.

Rob and Allan loaded our tack, bags, and bows into the truck, and I went to get Red since he and the sheep were going to share the bigger box stall at the front of the trailer. Maverick and Artimax would be loaded last.

Allan moved the trailer to the front of the larger barn since the ground was more level there and all the horses left their extra-early breakfasts to come out into their attached paddocks and stare excitedly at the oversized rig.

Rabbit, Pender's big thoroughbred, was closest and he kept tossing his head and calling loudly as if he expected new horses to appear from off the trailer at any second.

"Shh, it's too early for yelling," I told him, "we're just going on a short vacation and then we'll be back. You'll have to guard the place while we're away."

He snorted loudly, broke into a lofty trot around his paddock, and then charged back inside for more hay.

Portia and Antonio were eager to follow Red out of the paddock but they both balked at the sight of the trailer, and I had to load Red first and then get a bucket of grain to encourage them up the ramp. That did it, though. As soon as I shook the bucket they bolted inside and I left them exploring Red's box stall and undoubtedly stealing his hay.

"Good riddance," Hilary said, yawning into her coffee. She'd gotten up early to see us off but was still in her pajamas and a pair of slippers. She sat sideways on the golf cart, watching us pack.

"You do know that Portia is coming back, right?" I asked her, raising an eyebrow.

"Yeah, yeah, but I'm hoping she comes home better behaved."

Unlikely, I thought, but didn't say it. I knew that deep, very deep, down Hilary would miss Portia, too.

Maverick and Artimax loaded next. Maverick stomped up the ramp with his ears pinned and his nose pinched with disapproval. Getting up early to go on a road trip did not agree with him. I wondered how he'd react when he saw the ranch again.

Artimax was a seasoned campaigner and used to getting up for shows at all hours, so nothing fazed him much. He located his hay net and was already happily settled in before we'd even closed the doors.

"Right," Allan said, "we're all loaded then. Do a final check to make sure you have everything because once we hit the road, we won't be turning around."

Our bags and bows were in the back of the truck and I'd secured Oona's painting safely in the tack room with all our gear. It *looked* like we had everything.

"All set, Nori?" I said as she climbed slowly into the back seat.

"Yes, thank you." Her voice was quiet and I frowned.

"You all right?"

She nodded and gave me a tight smile. I wondered what was

bothering her. She had been so excited to go on this trip. I hoped she wasn't having second thoughts.

But it was too late to do anything about that by then.

"I'll miss you," Hilary said, wrapping me in a tight hug, "but don't worry, I'll take care of everything here and send you updates. I'll take good care of Caprice."

I hugged her back. Hilary and I had gone through a rough patch last year. But things seemed to have mended and I felt like we were on our way to being best friends again.

There were last minute hugs from Annie and then the truck rumbled to life and I hurriedly climbed in with Rob following close behind me.

The second the door slammed shut it was like someone had flicked a switch in my head, and I went from a flutter of nerves, doubts, and worries to just happy excitement. The decision had been made; there was no going back now. And only fun adventures lay ahead of us.

"Are you ready for this?" Rob said, reaching over to squeeze my hand.

"More than ready."

The truck lurched forward, turning a hard left until we were facing down the driveway again and then we were off.

CHAPTER 7

It was a sixteen-hour trip up to the ranch, including the ferry ride, and we varied from staring at the changing scenery, watching the horses on the trailer-cam, talking non-stop, and napping. I hadn't been on the ferry in over a year and I followed the others eagerly to the top deck, sniffing at the salty air appreciatively and leaning over the railing to stare at the frothy, white wake that slapped and foamed against the boat's metal hull.

There were no dolphins or whales to be seen this time, but there was a good wind so the sail boats were out in full force, leaning sideways into the waves, their sails stretched tight against the breeze.

The ferry swayed and lurched too in the swells and I felt my stomach rolling from side to side along with it.

"I hope the horses are okay," Nori said worriedly, voicing my concerns.

"We feel it up here more than they do below," Allan assured her. "And, look, there's the mainland already, it won't be so rough once we get closer."

I breathed a sigh of relief when I saw the land. I'd always had smooth sailings on the ferry before, although you heard stories about people being tossed around or the boat not being able to dock in the rough weather. It would take my stomach a while to stop feeling queasy again.

The horses were fine, of course; they were just eating their hay, not bothered at all by being below deck surrounded by a sea of parked cars and the stench of fuel.

"You're very good road trippers," I told them, reaching in to scratch under Red's chin. The sheep were curled up together in the far corner of their shared stall, calmly eating their hay and blinking at me with sleepy expressions.

There was a gentle bump and a lurch as the ferry docked and all around us car engines fired up, everyone eager to get on with their own adventures.

We drove for another couple of hours before stopping for lunch at a truck stop. Despite the depressing grey building topped with a half-burnt-out flickering neon sign, the parking lot was packed.

"Don't judge it by the outside," Allan said, noticing our skeptical looks. "This place has great food and clean bathrooms. Two important things when you spend all your days on the road."

It was certainly popular anyway. We had to wait near the front until our table was ready so I had plenty of time to soak up the unique atmosphere.

"This place looks like a crypt," Nori said darkly, and I could sort of see her point.

The walls were painted a lurid red that matched the red and black carpet and the vinyl bench seats in the booths. The tables were made of a black, shiny material that gleamed under the red stained-glass lamps overhead.

"It has character," Rob said, grinning at me.

"And the food smells amazing," I added as a server passed right by us with a tray overflowing with fragrantly steaming platters.

My stomach growled and I put a hand over it to make it shush.

Finally, our table was ready. Our waitress filled our coffee cups and slapped thick menus down on the table in front of us.

There was too much to choose from and it was early still, not quite breakfast and not quite lunch, so that sent me into a tailspin of indecision, too. But I finally settled on blueberry waffles.

It felt another age between when the waitress took our orders and finally dropped off our food, and when our plates actually, like some miracle, arrived we fell to eating like ravenous, starving wolves, not saying another word until we were scraping our plates and looking around for more.

"That was amazing," Nori said, using her last lone potato to scoop a dollop of hollandaise sauce off her plate.

"Told you," Allan said, looking amused. "Everything is made from scratch using old family recipes. They didn't get this popular for nothing."

We'd already checked on the horses before we'd eaten. Filling their nets and hanging up water buckets so they could relax with a drink while the trailer wasn't moving. Now we visited them one last time and took the half-empty buckets out so they wouldn't splash everywhere while we were driving.

"Halfway there, guys," I told them. Everyone but Maverick seemed content enough. He had his ears flattened, but that was pretty typical for him.

Tired from our early morning wake-up and full of delicious food, we all passed out nearly as soon as the truck started and didn't wake up again until we were nearly there.

I woke up and stretched my cramped limbs out, rubbing my cheekbone where it had been mashed up against the window.

"You're just in time," Allan said, smiling over at me.

Rob was still asleep between us, his head tilted back and his mouth slightly open. Even sleeping in the most awkward position possible, he still managed to look beautiful.

"I recognize this stretch of road," I said excitedly. "We're not far away at all. It looks so different than from when I came last time, though. It's so green."

This was the road that led from Triple Hills the town to Triple Hills the ranch. I'd had to ride this way every day on my way to and from school. Even some of the mailboxes looked familiar.

"Well, we're not in a drought this time. Not yet anyway. I think you'll find that a few things have changed around here," Allan said mysteriously.

"Oh, like what?"

"Well, you'll see soon enough, I guess. I can tell you one thing though, your Aunt Lillian was thrilled to stop running cattle. She had a little celebration on the day the last of them went to auction, and I happened to be in town. It was good to see her so happy."

"Yeah, I remember how much she disliked the cows."

"And then there's that dressage stuff ... but you probably know more about that part than I do."

I made a non-committal noise under my breath and turned to look out the window again, feeling a stab of guilt that I hadn't really made much of an effort to keep up with what had been happening here while I was gone. I talked to my aunt every few months or so, but she wasn't the biggest conversationalist and we usually ended up just talking about *me* and what was going on in my life.

Liza and Justin both sent me photos of the horses from time to time, and I'd kept tabs on what the archery team had been up to through Lincoln's infrequent emails, but beyond that I hadn't imagined that much had changed.

My first inkling was when Allan's big truck made the final turn off the highway and we drove down the long gravel road toward the ranch.

"Rob, wake up," I said, shaking his arm excitedly. And then harder when he didn't respond. "We're here."

He made some mumbling noises under his breath but he finally sat up and rubbed a hand across his eyes just as we reached the driveway. The red barn-shaped mailbox was still there but the rest of the entryway had had a makeover.

"Oh, the sign has changed," I said in surprise. The curved wooden tree trunks still arched high across the driveway, a bleached-out cow skull hanging between them in the middle where the two sides met. But now there were also two wooden barrels filled with colourful flowers. And beside the rustic wooden sign that had the Triple Hills brand burned into it there was another shiny red sign that read Triple Hills Equestrian Center. Beneath that was the drawn outline of three horses, one obviously a dressage horse, the next a western horse sliding to a stop, and the other was of a trail horse climbing between two mountains.

"Like I said, they've made a few changes here," Allan said, "all for the good, I think. It's nice to see it bustling and full of life again, like back when your uncle Trent was alive."

The rest of the driveway was just like I remembered, long and winding with crushed gravel crunching under our tires, and I felt another shiver of excitement ripple over me.

We're here, we're here, we're actually here, I sang inside my head. I turned to look at Nori to find her fully awake, staring out the windows with wide eyes.

We came to the fork in the driveway where two signs with arrows were posted in two identical flower barrels. The one on the left said "house" and the one on the right said "barns." The trailer swooped to the right and I held my breath, waiting for that moment when we'd come out of the trees and the whole ranch would lay sprawled out beneath us.

"Wow," Nori said, shifting over to get a better look at the shimmering lake down below and the miles of pastureland dotted with horses as far as the eye could see. "This is amazing."

Allan slowed a little so we could drink in the view. Last time

I'd arrived at the ranch, the hills had been brown and sunburnt, but now the fields were electric green and the grass waving next to the driveway was thick and plentiful. What a difference a season could make.

"There's the training barn," I said eagerly, pointing out the huge indoor arena that swung into view. Unlike last time I'd been here, the parking lot was full of cars and people were milling everywhere.

"They're having a sort of western fun day for some of the 4H kids," Allan said. "Your aunt was telling me about it last week. We're to put your horses in the broodmare barn."

"Nori, there's the archery range," I told her as we passed it, "over there on the left."

We all turned to peer at the long, low building that Lincoln and I, with the help of the rest of the school archery team, had converted from an old milking barn. It looked just like I remembered it except there were those barrels of flowers again and a small sign that said "Archery" next to the door.

By that time I was nearly bouncing on my seat with excitement, and when the broodmare barn came into view, it felt like I was coming home again. This barn was where Folly had lived when she'd first come to the ranch and I'd spent so many hours there working with her. And even more hours once the broodmares had come in for the winter to have their babies. We'd all spent countless late nights on foal watch. I'd seen some beautiful things there and some sad things, too. Red's mother, Beezy, had died shortly after giving birth to her new colt, and her death had hit everyone hard. She'd been one of Aunt Lillian's foundation mares and her favourite of the bunch.

I knew the mares and their young foals would already be out on pasture for the summer, getting fat and sassy on the lush grass. We would probably have the whole barn to ourselves.

The trailer hadn't even rolled to a stop before I'd opened my door and jumped out, my boots hitting the gravel with a satisfying thud. This was so much different than my arrival last time when I'd had a cast on my arm, bandages across my nose, and the certainty that I was never going to get on a horse again.

"Astrid!" Aunt Lillian appeared in the barn doorway, a cowboy hat on her head and a huge smile on her face. Her long silver braid had been cut short, to just above her shoulders and she looked younger, and much happier, than I remembered.

She was at my side and wrapping me in a tight hug before I could blink, and I hugged her back as hard as I could.

"It's so nice to see you, girl. You look good."

"You too," I said, "thanks so much for letting us come up here."

"Nonsense, this visit is way overdue. I'm happy to have you. I hope you'll like it so much that you'll decide to stay permanently."

She laughed as she said it but the look she gave me told me she meant it.

Truck doors slammed behind me and I remembered my manners.

"Aunt Lillian, you remember Rob."

"Of course I do. Couldn't forget a handsome face like that, especially when he's so good at selling my horses." She shook Rob's hand heartily before pulling him into a hug. "And you must be Nori."

She turned and smiled at Nori kindly.

"Yes," Nori said, suddenly awash in shyness again, "thanks for letting me tag along."

"Oh nonsense, I've heard about all the good work you've been doing with Maverick. I think you'll be a real asset to our team here. I can't wait to see that horse in action. He's a good horse, although not everyone can see that."

Nori lit up at the mention of her beloved and her shyness evaporated. "He's the best," she said, grinning, "he's not afraid of anything."

"Oh, I remember. Well, let's get these creatures unloaded and settled in the barn. Their stalls are all—" she broke off, catching sight of Allan, who was just now climbing out of the driver's side of the truck.

Leaving her sentence unfinished, she strode around to meet him. "Good to see you, Allan," she said in her booming voice. "Thanks for taking care of my crew here. I hope you're still going to take me up on my offer to stay for dinner."

She paused, looking at him with a hopeful expression. I couldn't see his face, since he was standing beside the truck out of view, but I did hear the warmth in his voice when he answered.

"Well, I don't want to put you to any trouble," he said.

"Nonsense, it's no trouble at all. We'd love to have you stay."

"Well, I don't think I can refuse your cooking, Lillian."

Their voices dropped and I turned away, feeling like I'd been eavesdropping.

"Come on," I said quickly to Rob and Nori, "let's see if the stalls are actually ready before we unload."

Walking into that broodmare barn I felt like a castaway who'd been shipwrecked and had just arrived home after decades away. There were no horses inside, but the air was hushed and cool and a few pigeons rustled on the thick wooden beams overhead. The sunlight filtered in from the high windows and dust motes drifted gently through the air.

"Oh wow, Astrid, I love this," Nori whispered. Which said something because she'd kept her horses in much fancier places all her life. There was just something comforting about this space, like it sort of enveloped you in peace the minute you walked inside.

Aunt Lillian *had* gotten the first three stalls nearest the door ready. Their wooden doors hung open and the interiors were deeply bedded with straw, water buckets filled and piles of fragrant hay heaped in each front corner. On the far wall of each stall were doors leading to their outside paddocks.

"They're going to enjoy living in this luxury," Rob said, looking impressed.

Allan and Aunt Lillian were still talking together when we went back outside so we just went to work unloading the horses ourselves. I unlatched the ramp and let it glide slowly to the ground before opening the interior trailer doors.

The horses inside whickered and one of the sheep *baaed*. I knew they would be glad to get out and stretch their legs after the long drive.

The first two backed out easily and stood blinking at their new surroundings. Maverick flattened his ears and then dove into a clump of nearby grass, not caring in the slightest that he was back on the ranch where he was born. Artimax probably just assumed he was headed to another show because he sauntered down the ramp like he'd only made a ten minute journey down and followed his friend leisurely to the grassy edge of the road.

"Hey, Red," I said, moving to his box stall. I led him out and had him stand still while I manoeuvered the door shut behind him. I'd have to come back for the sheep.

When he stepped out of the trailer, he stopped suddenly and then stood very still and quiet, his nostrils flaring as he sniffed at the air. His eyes widened, and then he threw up his head and let out a bugling neigh that nearly scared me half to death. I'd never heard him make a sound like that before; he was usually so laid back.

From far away another horse answered, and then another, and I wondered which of his friends were calling to him.

"It's okay buddy," I told him quietly, "we'll go find them tomorrow. It sounds like someone will be happy to see you."

He huffed the breeze a few more times and then heaved a big sigh and nudged my arm with his nose.

"Are you ready to go inside and check out your new home?"

Red followed Artimax into the barn, his hoofs scuffing quietly on the dirt floor, his ears pricked as he looked around with interest.

He nickered softly under his breath when he saw the hay in his stall and dove into it the second I had his halter undone.

"Glad you're not too stressed out," I said, laughing, "make yourself at home."

Rob had settled Artimax into the stall beside me and after a minute of snacking and exploring their new bedrooms the two horses marched through the doors at the back of each of their stalls and began checking out their new paddocks, sauntering along side by side with the fence between them.

Nori was still outside grazing Maverick and I took a moment to just breathe a sigh of relief. We'd made it safely, the horses were fine, and I had a whole month of fun and learning ahead of me.

Suddenly, the sound of outraged *baaing* broke the silence. Outside I heard Allan swear, and then both Portia and Antonio burst into the barn, hooves skidding on the dirt floor. Portia *baaed* anxiously again and Antonio did a little buck in the air, kicking out his hind feet.

"You're okay, guys," I called, opening Red's door. "Your home is over here."

Portia swung around and as soon as she saw me, her eyes lit up and she charged toward the safety of the stall, Antonio close on her heels. They skidded inside, sides heaving, eyes rolling but as soon as they caught sight of the hay pile and saw Red standing in the outside doorway they marched right up and began eating as fast as they could.

My aunt came striding back into the barn with an irritated look on her face. "That ram needs to get out on pasture with the other sheep first thing," she said firmly, "he *butted* Allan when he opened the door. Hard."

"Oh, I'm so sorry," I said quickly, "he does that sometimes. He's only playing."

"Well, it's a bad habit and it won't be cute once he's big enough to do some damage. They can be very dangerous when they're grown up, and the rams that have been made into pets are the worst. We'll have to keep an eye on him once he's older."

I bit my lip and stared down at Antonio with a sigh. He was getting to be more of a handful the older he got, everyone at the barn spoiled him with treats and he'd grown to expect food and attention from everyone.

"Don't worry about it too much, Astrid," she said quickly, seeing my expression, "once he's spent a season out on pasture with the ewes, he'll most likely calm down. They'll help put him in his place. Now, let's get this trailer unloaded."

It took us a while to ferry our things to the barn aisle and then Aunt Lillian strongly hinted that we should thoroughly clean out the dirty shavings in the trailer and hose it out since Allan had been nice enough to bring us all the way up here.

We were all exhausted from the long trip but fair was fair and there wasn't any point grumbling over it. Aunt Lillian and Allan disappeared somewhere while we got to work shovelling out the trailer, sweeping the floor and then spraying it down with the hose until it looked good as new.

The sun was headed firmly toward the horizon by the time we'd finished cleaning and had organized our things nicely in the tack room. I had set Oona's painting for Liza carefully off to one side where it wouldn't get knocked over.

"Ow, something bit me," Nori said, slapping her arm. "Oh my gosh, there's another one. What are those things?"

"Oh, right," It was all coming back. "Uh, the bugs are a little bigger here than back home."

That was a bit of a lie. The mosquitos were more than double the size of the ones that lived on the Island, and they were about ten times more bloodthirsty and aggressive. They descended on us in a growing swarm, whining around our ears and biting any exposed skin. Soon, we were slapping our arms and legs non-stop.

"Maybe we could leave our stuff here and come back for it later. It's not too long of a walk to the house or we could hike down to the training barn and see if maybe Liza or Justin are around. They could probably drive us back up to the house."

"Whatever gets us out of this mosquito storm," Nori said irritably, slapping at her neck. "They're awful."

Luckily, we were spared any walking by the rumble of a truck engine. I bounced up and down in delight, recognizing the white truck right away.

"Justin!" I called in excitement as he stepped out of the truck. He looked exactly the same as I remembered, all tall with chiseled features and laughing brown eyes.

He crossed toward me in a few strides and wrapped me in a tight hug, lifting me off the ground, twirling me around once and then dropping me again with a laugh. He smelled like horses, sweat, and leather.

He shook Rob's hand and said hello to Nori, who was staring at him open-mouthed.

"Come on, throw your stuff in the truck. Liza's just finishing her last lesson but I thought I'd run you all up to the house before I hit the showers. You've had a long trip."

We threw our things into the open back of the pick-up and clambered into the truck, gratefully shutting the doors against the whining drone of mosquitos.

Justin took the rutted short cut up to the house and we bounced along, too busy clutching the seats, the dashboard, or anything else to pay attention to the drive.

"Sorry, I took the fast and bumpy way. There you go." Justin said, jolting to a stop. "We'll be up for dinner as soon as we can. Don't eat everything before we get there."

"Thanks. I think," I said, easing myself gingerly out of the truck, amazed that I was still in one piece. I hated that shortcut just as much now as I had when I'd lived here.

But my spirits soared when I looked up at the big, familiar log house all warm and lit up from inside so it looked like a painting.

"This is where you *lived?*" Nori said, gazing at the house in awe. "Why did you ever decide to move away?"

And really, I was beginning to wonder that myself.

We unloaded all our things in record time, piling it all on the driveway so we could start the long process of ferrying it to the house.

I looked up as a shadow detached itself from the front porch and, with a low woof, a massive dog lumbered down the steps toward the car.

"Oh, Jake," I said happily, moving to meet him halfway and leaning down to scratch his wiry ears. I didn't have to lean far because the big Irish Wolfhound was nearly to my chest in height. His tongue lolled and he panted his gross dog breath on me happily. He looked a little older and he had a hitch in his step that hadn't been there before, but he recognized me and that was all that mattered.

"Whoa, you need a breath mint, dog," I teased him, giving him a gentle hug around the neck before I turned back to help the others with the luggage. We carried everything to the porch as fast as we could, dodging the terrier-sized mosquitos, and piled it all just inside the front door.

The smell of delicious food made my stomach grumble. It felt like it had been hours and hours since lunch.

"Oh, there you are," my aunt said, appearing from the kitchen wearing a black apron that went down to her knees. "I was beginning to wonder if you'd been eaten by bears. Right, Rob, you're in your old guest room on the main floor here. It's just that second door down the hall. I've got it all ready for you. And girls, you are upstairs. Astrid, I gave you your old bedroom and Nori, you'll be right beside her. Follow me, ladies."

Only the weight of my luggage kept me from skipping up the stairs. A bubble of happiness welled up in my heart and I could hardly contain it.

My room was just as I'd left it. The polished wooden logs, the plaid bedspread and curtains; it was small and cozy and made me feel safe. I remembered what I'd been feeling back when I'd arrived here last time. I'd been broken and scared and so lost but living at the ranch had brought me back to life.

I looked out the window into the dark woods, just making out the branches of the nearest trees. There was a small flash of yellow near the top of the pine closest to the house and suddenly I heard a haunting call. Whooo hoo hoo hoo.

An owl, my skin prickled and a sudden shiver rippled down my spine when I remembered seeing the owls in the forest back home. Rob had told me that historically owls represented wisdom and the coming of big changes. But I couldn't help thinking they were more ominous than that.

I'm being silly, I thought, *it's just a regular old owl doing its thing. It's not like it's a messenger from the underworld or something.*

Laughter brought me back to the present and I followed the sound out into the hall and into the room next door to mine. Nori and Lillian were sitting on the bed looking at a small photo book.

"Come see," Nori said, looking up with a genuine smile on her face. "It's Maverick."

I came over and sat down beside her, laughing too when I realized that it was a book of baby photos of a sulky little colt with his ears pinned as he tried to nurse from his mother.

"I'd forgotten that these were on my computer. He was such a funny, quirky little guy that we actually took quite a few of him at this stage. I sent them to the drugstore in town and they made them into a book for me. I thought Nori might like to have it. There he is as a two-year-old, still the same expression on his face, and this one was when he was started under saddle. Here, you keep it."

"For me?" Nori said. "Really?" She was looking up at Lillian adoringly, the book clutched to her chest.

"Of course, now you girls get washed up and changed. Dinner will be on the table in fifteen minutes so you don't have much time. Astrid, Bryce is bringing his girls over too, so you'll want to go down and catch up."

I hurried back to my room to quickly get changed out of my travelling clothes, have the world's fastest shower and run a comb through my hair. Bryce was the farm manager and had been the head trainer at the ranch back when I'd lived there, although I wasn't sure how that worked now since Justin and Liza had taken on such big roles. I'd gone to school with his daughter Casey, who had started off a bit quirky but had been decent in the end. I was looking forward to seeing them all again.

"Are you ready, Nori?" I called, knocking lightly on her door.

It took a minute for her to open it and she looked pale and nervous again, the laughter from Aunt Lillian's visit had already faded away.

"Hey, come on, let's go find Rob and get dinner. Don't worry, you're going to love it here."

"I'm not worried," she said quickly. "I'm fine." She sent me a tentative smile and brushed past me toward the stairs.

She'll settle in once we start riding, I thought, watching her tight back and hunched shoulders with a frown.

"Watch the stairs," I said just in time, Nori grabbed the handrail just as her socked feet slid on the polished wooden steps. I couldn't even count how many times I'd almost slipped on those steps back when I'd lived here.

"Thanks," she said, catching her breath, "those are lethal."

The scents coming from the kitchen were heavenly, and the voices rising and falling and the laughter brought me back in time to my first week here. I guessed that Nori might be feeling a little lost and scared like I had. I vowed to keep a close eye on her and make sure she was having a good time.

We went to find Rob first but his room was already empty, his suitcase unpacked and his clothes neatly hanging in the closet. Unlike my own room, which showed evidence of my whirlwind marathon to get ready for dinner. I'd left my over-packed suitcase sprawled open on my bed, the contents spilling out over the quilt and I'd yet to hang a single thing up. When it came to neatness, Rob and I were complete opposites.

We found him already looking at home in the kitchen, seeming completely at ease as he chatted with Liza and Justin. He looked up as we came in, meeting my gaze and smiling warmly so my heart gave a little lub-lub in my chest in response.

"Astrid," Liza said in excitement, catching sight of me, "it's so good to see you." She moved around the table to give me a hug and then stood back to look me over. "You look great, kiddo. And happy. I've heard all about your progress from Oona. She said you and Red are doing great."

"We're having fun," I told her, "but we haven't really been schooling properly or anything. We're just playing around."

"Well, I don't agree with that. Doing in hand and long-line work *is* schooling properly, actually. It's nearly a lost art that not many people make time for these days. You're going to find you're much further ahead than you think. Not that it's a race or anything," She added. "Everyone is on their own journey and I personally don't care if you ever choose to show again."

She paused for breath and then started to laugh. "There, you've only been here five minutes and I've already given you your first lecture. Sorry about that."

"She can't help herself," Justin added, throwing an arm around her shoulders. "She just can't keep all that knowledge to herself."

"Oh, bugger off," she laughed, pushing him away. "You're one to talk, anyway. Between the two of us it's a wonder we have any students left. It's a miracle we haven't bored them all to death by now."

I opened my mouth to protest because neither Liza nor Justin could *ever* be accused of being boring but Aunt Lillian clanked a spoon against her wine glass to get our attention.

"Five minutes, everyone. Time to set the table. Bryce and the girls will be here any second and this food is almost ready."

"Well, let me help with something, Lillian," Allan said from his seat at the far end of the table. He took a sip from his wine glass and beamed at her. "Allow me to work to pay for my supper."

"No, no, you just sit there," she said. "You're our guest today."

Lillian smiled and patted his shoulder as she passed him, a faint tinge of pink staining her cheeks.

Hmm, I thought, *this is getting very interesting.*

I set out the plates and cutlery while Nori did the glasses, and then Aunt Lillian put some flat wooden trivets on the table and we began setting out the dishes of steaming food.

And then the front door opened and a little girl ran in, her golden hair framing her heart-shaped face in two braids. It was Bryce's youngest daughter, Olive, looking much taller than I remembered. Her expression lit up when she saw me, and she barrelled over and wrapped me in a tight hug.

"Astrid, you're home!" she squealed.

"Oh my gosh, Ollie, you're all grown up. How did that happen?"

"I don't know,' she laughed, pulling away far enough to look up at me. "Did you see Salsa yet? She looks great; she loved California but she's happier here. We're going away to horse camp next week and I know she'll be the best horse there."

She turned and looked around the room, suddenly realizing that she had an audience. "Ooh, are you Astrid's boyfriend?" she asked, catching sight of Rob.

"Okay, Ollie, let's take it down a notch," Bryce said, coming in and laying a hand firmly on her head. He grinned at me and then pulled me into a hug. "Good to see you, kiddo. You saw your mare?"

"Not yet. We haven't had time but hopefully later tonight."

"Well, she's fat and sassy. Her foster colt, Figaro, is out with the other youngsters. We'll do a trail ride out to see them in the next couple of days and you can see him out with the herd. I popped in to see Red before I came over here. He looks good. You've done a great job with him."

"Thanks, I love him."

Suddenly, I caught sight of the slender figure behind him and broke into another grin. "Hey, Casey."

She'd let her dark hair grow out past her shoulders but she still looked like a miniature librarian with her cardigan sweater that she was inexplicably wearing in the summer, thick glasses, and intelligent expression. Casey was very smart but she'd had some trouble learning how to get along with people when I was there last. Now she looked much more happy and relaxed.

"Hey," she said, smiling at me shyly. "It's good to see you, Astrid. Did you hear I finally got into Redmond last year? I'm doing some really fun summer classes, too. I'm really excited."

"That's great, Casey." Redmond was a fancy private school she'd been trying to convince her dad to let her attend and it had nearly broken her heart when she hadn't gotten a full scholarship. I was glad she'd finally gotten to go.

We didn't have time to say much more than that before Aunt Lillian clapped her hands together loudly and announced that dinner was ready.

There was a moment of confusion while we scrambled for seats. I saw Nori heading for the chair beside me but Olive beat her to it and Nori was left near the end of the table between Casey and Bryce. She didn't look very happy about sitting next to strangers, either.

Dinner was great. I just concentrated on shovelling food in my mouth and listened to the lively chatter going on around the table. Rob was seated directly across from me and every now and then he looked up and sent me a grin. My heart was suddenly lighter and now that I was here a month seemed too short. I already didn't want it to end.

I had hoped that we'd have time after dinner to get away to see the training barn and the archery range. And maybe explore a little on our own. But after dinner there was coffee and dessert, and then everyone was having such a good time talking and listening to Allan's stories about his life on the road that it seemed rude to leave.

And by the time everyone was heading out, I was rubbing my eyes and yawning with sleep and only wanted to quickly do one last check on the horses and go to bed. Nori had already fallen asleep tucked up at one end of the couch, and Olive had curled up on Jakes dog bed beside him and had done the same thing.

"We'd better go feed while we still can," Rob said, reaching his hand out to pull me up out of the leather arm chair I'd tucked myself into.

"Now, you kids don't be walking around in the dark on your own," Aunt Lillian warned, "there are bears and cougars out there for sure. Astrid, your truck keys are on the rack, right where they always are."

Right, I thought excitedly, *I almost forgot about that.*

"We have our own transportation," I told Rob gleefully.

I pulled the keys off the rack by the front door and went to find my old friend.

"Here she is," I said proudly, pointing at the battered blue truck I remembered so fondly.

"I think there are even more dents than last time," Rob said with a laugh.

"Yep, oh and the back seat is filled with dog hair and tack again, Lillian obviously hasn't cleaned it once since I've been gone."

The truck had been filthy when I'd taken it on the first time, and I'd spent days scrubbing it clean and removing all the hair from the upholstery, trying to get the interior to stop smelling like a wet dog.

"Well, you have a month to spruce it up to your exacting standards," Rob said, grinning.

The engine lugged to life after a few tries and we rolled down the driveway under a blanket of stars.

The horses whickered sleepily when we slipped into the barn and one of the sheep let out a low *baa*.

Everyone still had hay, but we topped them up and made sure their waters were full and that everyone had settled in.

They all looked just as tired as we felt.

Yawning and rubbing our eyes we headed back up to the ranch house. We just had enough energy for one sleepy kiss goodnight and then both of us stumbled off to our beds.

CHAPTER 8

There was one confused, panicked moment in the chilly hours of dawn when I woke up thinking I was back home. Not at the Ahlbergs' or at my aunt's, but at that cold, sterile condo where I'd spent most of my life back before I'd run away. That feeling of seeping dread that I'd experienced every morning I'd woken up there stole over my body, freezing me with fear. It only lasted a few seconds but it brought back a host of painful memories that I couldn't quite shake even once I'd realized where I was.

You're safe, you're fine, I told myself, burrowing deeper under the covers, but it took a few minutes for my heart to stop thudding and my breathing to go back to normal.

There was no falling back asleep after that and finally, I rolled out of bed and unzipped the large suitcase I'd shoved to the floor last night without bothering to unpack.

I'll sort all this out as soon as I get back from the barn, I promised myself, rifling around inside until I found something decent to wear.

The pale sky outside the window was streaked with pink by the time I was ready.

Good enough, I thought, suddenly eager to be outside and see the ranch waking up.

I slipped into the hall, tip-toeing to Nori's room first to listen at her door. It was all quiet so I didn't bother knocking.

I coasted down the hall, pausing at the little library nook at the top of the stairs for just a minute, remembering all the peaceful hours I'd spent there, curled up with a book in front of the fireplace.

Downstairs the house was completely quiet except the floorboards creaking now and then under my feet. I paused at the front door, wondering if I should wake Rob up.

Let him sleep in, I thought finally. *He was so tired last night and I'll have plenty of time to show him the place later.*

A cool mist lay across the ground outside and the thick grass was heavy with dew. I would have to stay right in the middle of the trail or my feet would be soaked through in five minutes.

Gravel crunched under my feet as I headed down the driveway. The shortcut from the night before was much nicer on foot than it was by vehicle and I inhaled deeply, taking in the fresh smells of damp grass and damp pine. Up ahead was the low, wooden bridge and already I could hear the creek rushing under it. I paused when I got there and leaned over the railing to stare at the churning water below.

I remembered that this creek had many faces; sometimes it was the slowest of trickles barely flowing through the narrow gully. Other times it was a raging torrent that nearly reached the height of the bridge. Right now it was somewhere in the middle. The water flowed powerfully over the rocks, making little waves and whitecaps where the water collided with fallen branches or boulders. Experimentally I picked up a stick and tossed it over, moving quickly to the other side to watch its progress. But there was no sign of it, the water had already grabbed the thin wood and sucked it under, swirling it away in a whirlpool current.

I wouldn't want to fall in there this time of year. I shivered and continued toward the barn, listening to the woods waking up around me. One bird chirped sleepily and then another. Suddenly, where there had been silence, the trees were full of birds, singing, calling, chattering until the whole forest was alive with noise. A pair of rabbits hopped out in front of me, sitting in the middle of the road on their haunches for a second before a sharp cracking sound in the woods behind them, like branches snapping, sent them bolting into the brush on the other side of the road.

I stopped too, holding my breath and listening hard, wondering what sort of animal was heavy enough to break branches. And when the sound didn't come again, I hurried onward to the barn without stopping.

To my surprise, the barn door had been rolled back already and the horses were munching their hay. Well, Red, Artimax, and the sheep were eating but Maverick's stall door hung open and he was gone.

Tamping down the bubble of panic I felt, I went to the makeshift tack room and saw that his saddle and bridle were gone. So at least he hadn't escaped or been stolen or anything.

She's probably just gone on a quick trail ride, I thought. But I was worried. There were thousands of acres of land to get lost on. How would we ever find her if she'd fallen off and was lying hurt somewhere? It could take days to locate her. What would I tell her mother?

I looked over at Red, wondering for a second if I should saddle up and go looking for her.

"What do you think, boy?" He snorted and lifted his head, staring at me with his kind, mild gaze. His jaws worked rhythmically on a giant mouthful of hay. One of the sheep let out a contented *baa* and I knew that it was time to just calm down and wait a little bit. Nori would probably come back on her own safe and sound.

To distract myself, I grabbed my brushes from the tack room

and went to work on Red's coat. He was usually pretty shiny and clean but he had obviously discovered some mud at the back of his paddock because one side of him was caked in a dried crust of grey earth.

"Antonio, stop that," I said as the oversized lamb butted my grooming tote with his head, "that's not food."

He wrinkled his nose and lowered his head again, eyeing up my brushes with a glint in his eye.

"No, Antonio," I said firmly, reaching down to tip his nose up and scratch his chin. The devilish look in his eye disappeared instantly and he tilted his head sideways so I could reach behind his ears. He was such a sucker when it came to attention. Portia came up beside him for her turn and I was stuck for another five minutes scratching until they finally got bored and went back to their hay.

"You guys are a full time job," I told them as I began running the curry comb over Red in little circles. He snorted happily as I worked the dirt from his coat and soon he was shiny and clean again. He looked calm and relaxed and did not seem at all stressed by his long trip the day before.

I took him out for a hand walk and to let him graze a little along the edge of the driveway. He sauntered along, working his way from tuft to tuft of greenery, looking for the choicest bits. There was still no sign of Nori by the time I'd returned. So I put Red back with the sheep and slowly picked out all three stalls and paddocks.

I might as well head back to the house and let Aunt Lillian know that she's missing, I thought when there was nothing left to do, *there's no point in me going out and looking since I hardly remember the terrain.*

And, as per usual, I was starting to get hungry.

The sun was well up by the time I made it back to the house and the second I opened the front door, the smell of frying food hit me and my mouth began to water. I pried my boots off and padded into the kitchen, which was already full of people. Liza and Justin were seated at the table side by side with a calendar and a notebook spread out between them. Rob sat across from them, still looking tousled with sleep, and was leaning across the table looking at whatever they were studying.

To my surprise, Allan was at the stove frying hash browns beside my aunt who was poking at the pan of bacon with a pair of tongs. I knew he'd stayed over in one of the downstairs guest rooms, but I'd thought he was leaving first thing.

"Hey," Rob said, looking up as I slid into the seat next to him. "Thanks for letting me sleep in. I haven't done that in a while."

"I don't think I've ever seen you sleep in," I said, resting my head against his shoulder for a second. He smelled freshly showered and clean and it was a few seconds before I remembered about Nori.

"Maverick's missing," I said, "I'm pretty sure Nori has him out riding somewhere."

"Well, of course she does," Lillian said, overhearing me. "Didn't you see the note on the table when you got up? She went riding with Casey and Mara. They drew a map and said they'd be back in a few hours. It shouldn't be much longer."

"Mara? Like archery Mara? Did she trailer over before dawn or something? How did they even meet each other?"

Mara had been one of the best shooters in our archery club but she'd also been a bit of a thug and there had been some bad blood between her and Casey over a horse. But they'd made up eventually and Mara had bought Aunt Lillian's own horse Kitty, who was a powerful little dark blue roan mare.

"That's a lot of questions before coffee, sweetie," Aunt Lillian said. "I suppose Casey set it up last night over dinner. Mara and her horse didn't trailer over; they are staying here at the ranch for the summer. She's living in the bunk house over the broodmare barn although I would have preferred that she move in here into the main house. I don't like her staying up there all alone.

"Now, I wouldn't worry at all about Nori while she's with Casey and Mara. Those girls have level heads on their shoulders and they both know this ranch inside out. They won't get lost."

I silently absorbed this information. I had so many questions to ask but before I could formulate the right ones, Aunt Lillian shoved a plate of scrambled eggs, bacon, and toast into my hands.

"Eat," she said, ruffling my hair a little as she went by. "We have a lot of work to do today. The countdown to this crazy event is on."

"We're just going over the schedule and the list of riders for the clinic, Astrid," Liza said, picking up her coffee cup and taking a long sip. "There are fifteen riders including you, Rob, and Nori. Seven of the riders have their own horses that they are bringing. So that leaves us with five riders who will be leasing ranch horses for the week. Our next step is to figure out which horses to use."

"I had Bryce bring them all in off the range a few days ago. They'll need a visit from the farrier and a good grooming." Lillian said. "They should be ready to go in no time."

"Well, a few of them might need a tune-up," Justin warned. "They've been out of work for almost a year. They might need to be reminded of their jobs."

"Oh, they won't be any trouble, I'm sure," my aunt said, turning back to the stove.

Justin exchanged a glance with Liza and shook his head.

Jake woofed from his spot beside the table as the front door banged open and Nori, Casey, and Mara trooped in looking dusty, exhausted and very happy.

"Thanks to whoever cleaned my stall," Nori said, heading straight toward the food. "I thought I was going to have to do that when I got back. I am so starving."

"Wash your hands first, girls. Did you have a good ride?" Lillian asked.

"Oh, yeah," Nori detoured to the sink without arguing. "Seriously, this place is awesome. We went right up to the top of a mountain where we could see the whole ranch spread out below, and off in the distance there was the town and a lake. It looked like a painting. Maverick loved it."

Her voice grew muffled as she stuffed some eggs into her mouth and flopped into the seat beside me. It was good to see her looking so happy. I hadn't seen her smile like that in months.

"Hey, Allan," Casey said, pulling up a chair beside him. "Where are you headed to next?"

"Off to Saskatchewan right after breakfast," Allan said. "This one will be a bit of a long haul, but I think I'll be back in this area in a few weeks."

"Well, you make sure to drop in and say hello," Lillian said, "you know you're always welcome here."

Mara had followed Casey and Nori to the table and she slowly pulled out the chair on the other side of me as if she were not quite sure of her welcome. Which was surprising because back when I knew her, she'd been the type of girl who had just demanded people made room for her without hesitation.

She looked different though, and not just because she'd cut all her hair off and gotten an eyebrow piercing. She looked older and also quieter, like life had beaten her down a little.

"Hey, Mara," I said, "good to see you. Are you still doing archery?"

"Yeah," she said, nodding. "I shoot all the time."

"That's great. Are you doing the archery clinic then?"

"Yes… um, well I think so." She shot a hesitant glance at Aunt Lillian.

"Well, of course she is," my aunt said. "Mara's the one responsible for getting the ball rolling on Mr. Belko's clinic in the first place. She is a real asset to this ranch and I don't know how we could manage without her."

Mara blushed furiously and looked down at the table.

I wonder what this is all about, I thought curiously.

"Great, we're all here now," Justin said, smiling around the table at everyone. "Girls, we were just talking about how we're going to pick out the ranch horses that we need for the clinic and get them tuned up in time. I think most of that is going to have to be your team's project, Astrid, because Liza and I still have sales horses to ride and lessons to teach. And my dad, Mara, and Casey have lots of chores to do. The ranch is in full swing right now and we'll be going non-stop all summer. So we'll need you to take charge of most of the preparations once we have the horses picked out."

"Sure, that's no problem," I said, glancing at Rob for confirmation.

"Yeah," Rob agreed, "between us we should be able to have them all ready in no time. They're already well-trained, right? They just need to get used to the archery stuff?"

"Um, well, mostly," Justin said. "They might be a little, er, rusty. They haven't been used in a while, but I'm sure it will all go smoothly."

"What are the people like who will be riding them?" Rob asked. "Are they beginners or more experienced?"

"A mixture really," Liza frowned as she ran her finger down the list of riders. "We have two that have never ridden before at all which should be interesting and then one that says he's very experienced and then two that have their own horses but couldn't bring them."

She pushed the list across to us and I scanned the page.

"Oh, that's Lincoln and Ally from the archery club," I said excitedly. "I really liked them. I knew Ally liked horses but I didn't think Lincoln did."

"Well, his father told me that Lincoln's only coming as a favour to his girlfriend. He's actually really nervous around horses. I guess Ally's parents signed her up as a present for her birthday and she talked Lincoln into going along."

"That's so sweet," I said. "What a nice boyfriend. They were both great people, I'm glad they're dating."

"Dating is highly overrated," Nori said around a mouthful of food. "In my brief experience, it sucked."

"Yeah, no kidding," Mara agreed.

"It's not like that when you're going out with someone who is actually a decent human being, Nori," I said.

She sent me a pointed glare across the table and I stopped myself from launching into my usual anti-Jackson speech.

"Moving on," Liza said, "the instructor, I mean Laszlo Belko, has it all organized really well anyway. He said we're starting everyone off exactly the same way no matter what their experience level. They start on the ground, and then they move up to that barrel horse thing, and then from a real horse at a standstill, and then with someone leading. They have to graduate from each stage before they can move on."

"That sounds great. What's the barrel horse, though?"

Liza and Justin exchanged a look and began to laugh.

"You'll see," Justin said. "We haven't actually figured out how to build it yet, but you can be the first to try it out once it's ready."

The smirks on their faces made me think that I would be avoiding any barrel horse at all costs.

"Will you come watch Folly's workout this morning?" Liza asked, meeting my gaze across the table.

"Oh, yes, definitely. And Oona gave me a present to bring to you. I'm supposed to be there when you open it. And I'd really like to see Quarry, too. When can we come?"

"Right after breakfast. But Quarry is turned out on pasture right now; Marcus, too. They're enjoying a short vacation."

She must have seen my expression fall because she hurried on. "We'll take a ride out to see them in their pasture soon. If not today then tomorrow. I promise. He's doing great."

As soon as breakfast was over, all of Aunt Lillian's regular staff headed off to start their long workday while the rest of us loaded the dishwasher, wiped down the table, and dealt with the pans on the stove.

Allan and my aunt had gone to the living room to finish their coffee and as soon as we could Rob, Nori, and I slipped out and climbed into the truck.

"Come see the archery range first," I said, "I've been dying to show it to you."

The truck shuddered to a stop in front of the low building, coughing for a few seconds even after I'd shut off the engine.

"Not a word," I said to both my passengers since they were sending doubtful glances toward my beautiful truck. "Just come check out our range."

"Wow, Astrid, this is so neat," Nori said as soon as we stepped inside. "I can't believe you did this all yourself."

I looked around the whitewashed walls with a feeling of pride. Not much had changed since I'd last been there. But it had been kept clean and nice and some of the targets had been replaced.

"Well, lots of people helped. Lincoln and Mara were there right from the beginning and then the rest of the archery club and the society people helped, too. And Aunt Lillian donated the space, of course."

I thought back to how the musty old barn had looked before, covered in a decade's worth of grime and spider webs. It had not been fun to clean it up but the end product had been worth it.

"I'd love to have my own range at home," Nori said dreamily. "Imagine how good I'd be if I could shoot every single day. You were so lucky."

Yeah, I thought, *I guess I was.*

We left my truck at the range and walked the short distance to the training barn.

Nori stopped, open-mouthed, in the barn doorway, staring up at the wooden log beams overhead and the bank of skylights that filtered in the soft morning light.

Rob had seen the barn before but even he was impressed.

"Wait until you see the arena," I told Nori. "My Uncle Trent was really into cattle penning and roping, so the ring had to be oversized so they could run cows around in there. They built it to host competitions and things, so it's huge."

The gate to the indoor was a see-through pipe-rail fence, and beyond it I caught a brief glimpse of a figure cantering by on a dark horse decked out in a black saddle and a white pad.

The horses in the barn were still eating their breakfast but they popped their heads up one by one when they heard us come in.

"Oh, look at this guy," Nori said, moving over to the first stall where a large golden horse with black points stood with his head over the door. He had huge jowls and large, soulful eyes. His long black forelock hung down almost to his nose.

"That's Doc," Justin said, appearing out of the tack room with a heavy western saddle slung casually over one shoulder by the horn. "He's one of our stallions, go on in and say hi; he's as friendly as they come."

Nori disappeared instantly into the big stallions' stall, and I could hear her crooning softly to him. Some stallions had reputations for being mean but I'd never met one like that. Aunt Lillian's stallions were the sweetest and most gentle horses, and Doc most of all.

"He is Possum's dad," I reminded Rob. "I wonder if there's another young horse out of him that you could take home for your project."

"Oh, there are plenty to choose from," Justin said, shaking his head a little. He went into a stall a few doors down from Doc where a stocky palomino stood patiently waiting with its saddle pad already in place. Justin swung the saddle in an easy arc and settled it lightly on the horse's back. "This guy is sold already and he leaves at the end of the week. I'm just keeping him tuned up for his new owner and giving him more experience on the trails.

But the second he leaves, there will be another one to move inside. We're swamped right now and the longer they sit the less chance they have of finding the right home."

He looked like he wanted to say more but instead he gave the horse a scratch behind the ears, slipped the bridle on and led him out into the aisle.

I knew how much Justin and his family liked Aunt Lillian. This was the closest he'd ever come to saying anything negative about how she ran the ranch, but I could see the frustration in his eyes.

Rob and I shared a glance.

"Hey, this is the one Mara rode on our trail ride today," Nori said, pointing at a little bay who was sleepily picking at his hay pile.

"He's cute. She didn't ride Kitty?" I asked.

"Nope." Nori shrugged. "She did say that she has her own horse but to tell you the truth she didn't say too much. Casey and I did most of the talking. But she showed us some really neat trails. They are so lucky to have grown up here."

"This is Fox," Rob told Nori as the big chestnut abruptly stuck his nose over his stall door, "this is the one that Liza is competing with right now."

"Ooh, he's fancy," Nori said, running a hand down the horse's neck.

Hooves thudded in the indoor and I saw another flash of the dark horse, actually a dark blue roan, dressed in white leg wraps and a white saddle pad. And there was Liza's familiar voice calling out instructions. I left Rob and Nori visiting with Fox as I drifted down toward the indoor, frowning at the horse and rider pair as they cantered past again. Something was familiar about them and yet ... suddenly it came to me.

Mara, barrel-racing, rough-talking, slightly scary Mara who had threatened to beat me up in front of a cafeteria full of people was now cantering around in elegant serpentines on her ranch horse Kitty, who had been transformed somehow into the most adorable dressage horse. Her mane was neatly pulled, her legs wrapped in white polos that matched her saddle pad, and there were sparkly blue rhinestones on her brow band that brought out the highlights in her shiny blue coat.

I would never have believed it if I hadn't seen it with my own eyes.

"Hey, Astrid," Liza called out happily, catching sight of me. "Come on in. I'm going to ride Folly next. Did you go visit her already?"

"No. Was she in this barn? I totally missed her."

Mara looked up, startled, from her serpentine, and Kitty abruptly swapped leads so she counter-cantered through the next loop.

"That's okay," Liza said, switching her gaze quickly back to Mara, "just refocus her. Good. Actually, you might as well let her walk now, Mara. She's done a lot today."

Mara made a face and moved Kitty into a loose-reined walk and brought her toward us, her expression guarded. I hoped she didn't blame me for shortening her lesson.

"Hey, Mara," I said tentatively. "So you switched to dressage, hey?"

"Looks like it," she said shortly, shrugging and looking away. Mara had never been an overly friendly person and she'd never been much of a talker.

"Well, you guys look really good."

Her guarded expression softened and she reached down suddenly to pat Kitty's neck. "Um, thanks."

"These two have worked really hard all winter," Liza said proudly. "They're a good team."

"Thanks," Mara said again, her ears turning pink. "Thanks for the lesson, Liza. I've got to get back to work."

"Okay, good job out there."

"See you," she said, shooting me a tentative smile.

"Bye, see you around."

"Don't mind her," Liza said, squeezing my arm. "She's sweet underneath. She had a really rough year, but she's a hard worker and a good rider."

"Aunt Lillian said she's living at the ranch for the summer?" I asked curiously. I was still trying to wrap my head around the idea of Mara as a dressage rider.

"Ah, yes, her parents had a bit of a falling out with her unfortunately and she had to leave home. She works so hard in exchange for living here and for Kitty's board and she made a deal with Lillian to help her out with the clinic fees. Don't tell her I said this but I think she could actually use a friend, someone on her side. Maybe you guys could include her in your plans sometimes."

"Yeah, of course. No problem."

"Thanks, Astrid. Now let's go find Folly. I can't believe you walked right past her."

"I know." I laughed. "She's going to kill me."

I followed Liza back into the aisle, scanning the stall doors eagerly. All the horses were busy eating so it took me a minute to find the chestnut head I was looking for. I reined in my excitement when I caught sight of her. Much like Mara, Folly was not one for enthusiastic outbursts.

I walked slowly to her stall and leaned over the door, taking in her glistening coat and well-muscled body. She looked fit and very happy.

"Hey, Folly," I said softly. "How are you doing?"

She popped her head up and took a good look at me, her ears pricked and her jaws working on a mouthful of hay. She stared and then suddenly made a small nickering sound under her breath and waded through her straw bedding toward me.

I held my breath when she nosed me softly, touching my arm and then my cheek without a hint of aggression. All traces of her old, angry self were gone and replaced by a sweet and gentle horse I barely recognized.

"Oh, Liza, she looks great. Is she really completely sound now?"

"More or less. She still needs massage and the chiropractor fairly steadily, but she's coming along really well. I have to get up before dawn usually to ride my own horses. But I saved her until last today so you could watch her work. This place has really taken off and it's gotten crazy busy around here."

"The ranch looks amazing."

"Thanks, we work hard on it. Oh, Rob, this is perfect timing," she added as she caught sight of him and Nori. "We have quite a few prospects for you to look at this time. I know Lillian is hoping you'll take one or two. Or twelve." She burst out laughing.

"Someone will have to build me a bigger barn if I'm going to take on that many horses," Rob said, raising his eyebrows. "And Astrid's going to have to start pulling her weight a little more in the riding department or I won't be able to keep up.'

"Hey," I said, pretending to be offended, "I sold my project horse before you sold yours."

It slipped out before I had a chance to think about it and I froze as soon as the words left my mouth.

There was a moment of silence. Rob's expression fell for a second and then he draped an arm around my shoulders and gave me a squeeze, already forgiving me before I'd forgiven myself. "Yes, you did. Is there anything you need help with here, Liza? We can do some riding for you, if you like."

"Yeah, I pretty much need ten more riders to keep up," she laughed. "But you're going to have your hands full just getting the ranch horses ready for archery. It's going to be a bigger job than you think."

We helped Liza brush and tack up Folly. Inside, I was bubbling with excitement although I tried to keep a lid on it because Folly did not enjoy high-energy outbursts, or at least she hadn't back when I'd owned her.

We went and sat on the bleachers to watch Liza ride and my heart lub-lubbed in my chest with pride and joy. Even though it had been partly my fault that Folly had been damaged in the first place, I had spent a lot of love, care, and hard work to rehab her. And it had been an incredibly proud moment when I'd handed over her papers to Liza.

Folly had first been a hostile stranger to me, then an enemy, then a teacher and then finally, a friend. Reuniting her with her true owner was the best thing I could have done.

Folly moved for Liza in a joyful way she never had for me, her eyes bright and her neck lightly arched, powerful hind legs propelling them along. Liza's expression was full of happiness too, and I knew all over that I'd made the right decision to give Folly to her.

Rob laced his fingers through mine and I knew he was thinking the same thing. He'd been there when both Folly and I had been at our absolute rock-bottom worst so he knew what a complete transformation this was.

"Isn't she amazing?" A voice said nearby and I turned to see that Mara had reappeared and was half-perched next to Nori at the edge of the bleachers as though poised to leave at any second. She'd changed from her breeches back into jeans and looked like her old cowgirl self again.

"That is a really nice horse," Nori said, shaking her head as Folly trotted by.

"Did you know that she used to be Astrid's old horse?" Rob asked her.

"Wow, really?" she said incredulously. "You gave up *that* for *Red*?"

"What do you mean? Red is perfect," I said, feeling a burst of protective outrage for my best friend.

"Um, yeah, sure, but he's not *that*." She pointed over to where

Folly and Liza were at the far end of the arena executing a flawless half-pass in our direction.

"No, that's true," I said slowly, smiling despite myself. Nori couldn't know that it was Liza's brilliant riding that shaped and contained all the powerful, sometimes furious, energy that was Folly.

I guess that's what makes great riders great. I thought, *the fact that someone from the outside thinks that it looks easy.*

"Actually, Red is pretty fancy," Rob said, frowning, his grip on my hand tightening a little. "He's a nice mover and he actually does some really solid collection work. He's a good horse."

Both Nori and I looked at him in surprise, startled at his suddenly serious tone.

"I never said he wasn't a good—"

She broke off as Folly cantered past us, snorting and tossing her head like a war horse as she powered out some three and then two time lead changes.

"Wow," Nori whispered under her breath and then sat in rapt silence.

It was like watching a painting come to life and we all sat there, frozen, as Liza worked the mare. Not a single one of us said another word until she was done.

"That's it for today," Liza called, letting the mare walk on a loose rein. Folly changed direction immediately and strode toward us. Folly never ambled, she moved in the long, purposeful, ground-eating walk of a predator. Her eyes fixed on us.

"Hey, Folly," I said, delighted that she'd zeroed in on me and come to nuzzle my pockets and rub her foamy mouth on my arm. She snorted happily, spraying us all to a chorus of laughter and disgusted groans from Nori. I scratched her underneath her throatlatch in that spot between her jaws that always got itchy. She half-closed her eyes and tilted her head sideways so I could dig my fingers in.

"She sure remembers you," Liza said, grinning as she vaulted to the ground. "Folly never forgets a friend."

"Or her enemies." I added. "I'm glad I'm on her friend list now. She really does look fantastic, Liza. And I'm no expert but she looks totally sound."

"Pretty close anyway. We've spent a lot of time building her up and conditioning her. So far she's progressing in her training in leaps and bounds. I just play with her and I don't push her. We're starting a winter show series here at the ranch this year so I'll enter her in a few classes to see how she does. If it doesn't stress her out then we'll look for some bigger shows to take her to."

"Is there enough interest around here in dressage to do a show series?" Rob asked thoughtfully.

"We think so, you'd be surprised how many people appeared out of the woodwork when I started teaching lessons. It's something interesting to do and every horse can happily compete at the lower levels. We'll have western dressage classes too, and those always attract a lot of entries.

Besides, the winters are long here so there's not much else for horse-people to do. As long as we make it fun then people will come."

I nodded thoughtfully, wondering if that was something we might be able to do back home at Hilary's farm. We'd gone to a few local shows but it was always such a hassle to trailer everyone over in shifts and then cart them all back at the end of the day.

It would be a good way for Hilary to attract business to the barn and her dad could even do the catering.

"Want to cool her out for me, Astrid?" Liza asked, jumping to the ground and loosening Folly's girth. "Then I can grill Rob about how Ferdi's coming along. Too bad you couldn't have brought him with you, too."

"Sure," I said, happily taking Folly's reins and leading her around the arena. She followed along peacefully beside me, nothing like the fire breathing dragon she'd acted like last year.

"Can I pet her?" Nori appeared beside me, her cheeks flushed.

"Of course you can," I said, looking at her in surprise. Nori rarely asked permission to do anything and I didn't quite understand the starry expression on her face as she reverently ran her hand down Folly's sweaty shoulder.

Nori was surrounded by a dozen beautiful, well-bred horses at the farm and I had never seen her interested in anyone but Maverick. And it had been his awful personality that had drawn her to him, not his looks.

Folly didn't want to stand still and be petted, she tugged on the reins impatiently, wanting to move, ever restless even after a full work-out and Nori fell into step beside us.

"I never actually minded dressage," she said out of the blue. "Lumi liked it, too. He was a chestnut, just like her."

I glanced over at her quickly, surprised that she was volunteering any information about Lumi, the horse she'd had before Maverick. He'd been a young event horse who'd had a freak accident while galloping and had to be put down. That had all happened before I'd met her, but I knew that she'd taken his loss very badly. She'd blamed herself for his accident and had nearly given up riding completely. She rarely talked about him and when she did, it usually put her in a dark mood that could last for days.

"Were they a lot alike?" I asked cautiously, wondering where this was going.

She nodded slowly. "I know I pretend to hate everything but trail riding and horse archery." She took a deep breath. "But I'm kind of missing my old life a bit. I miss training hard and schooling. I miss jumping."

I sighed inwardly, looking for the right words to say. This is what Rob had been worried about when she'd wanted to buy Maverick, that she'd change her mind and eventually want a fancier, more competitive horse, like the type she'd been used to riding before.

"I'm not talking about giving up Maverick," she snapped, somehow guessing my thoughts. "Why does everyone think I'm going to dump him? He's more versatile than you think anyway, and he's been much more willing lately. I've been jumping him at home a bit—" She broke off, a faraway look on her face.

"You have?" I stopped short on giving her a lecture about jumping without supervision. It wasn't the time. "How did he like it?"

"He liked the jumps on the trail just fine once he figured out what I wanted him to do. He wasn't so thrilled about the ones in the ring."

I laughed under my breath, imagining what the scene must have looked like. He'd probably knocked every single rail down on purpose. Out of spite.

"I'm going to ask Liza to give me some lessons," she said defiantly, as if I were going to try and talk her out of it. "I have my own money. I can pay her."

"Um, okay," I said neutrally, keeping a straight face. "I'm sure she would be fine with that."

"It won't get in the way with me helping out here. And I don't want my mom to know. She'll get all excited and pushy. I want to do this on my own."

"That's fine with me," I said, although privately I thought any troubles Nori had with her mother were in her own head. Annie was a saint and she bought her kids whatever they wanted and loved and supported them with a fierce protectiveness that I envied completely.

"Thanks," Nori said stiffly. She gave Folly a final pat on the shoulder and then strode off toward where Liza and Rob were still talking, her back rigid with determination.

"That is one strange child," I whispered to Folly, running a hand down her neck and across her chest to make sure she was cooling properly. Her sweaty coat was almost dry. "But if anyone can turn Maverick into a show-pony, it's her. I've never met anyone more stubborn."

Folly nudged me sharply in the arm, and I stopped and moved her firmly out of my space before continuing our walk. She was the type of horse that needed to know her boundaries or she would walk all over you in a heart-beat. "Okay, you're right, you are pretty stubborn, too," I said laughing.

We were alone in the arena by then and since her coat was dry, I led her slowly back to the barn, enjoying the feeling of being with her again without the pressure of having to ride her. As much as I admired her, I wouldn't ever want to go back to those nightmare days of owning her again.

Folly's hooves clopped down the aisle as I led her to the set of cross-ties where Liza was waiting with her halter.

"You two look good together," she said. "Sure you wouldn't like to take her for a spin?'

"Nope," I said, laughing. "But I'll put her away for you."

I gave Folly a bath just like old times, scraped her down and let her hand graze until she was dry.

"Come on, Astrid," Nori called impatiently from the barn. "You're taking forever. We need to go see the archery horses. Aren't you dying to meet them?"

She didn't look quite so enthusiastic when Justin led us down to a big grassy paddock behind the training barn, and we stared at the bedraggled group of half-neglected ranch horses waiting for us.

They weren't thin or anything. But their feet were a little long and they obviously had not been brushed in ages. Worst of all, their long manes, tails, and forelocks were tangled in massive, prickly knots.

"What on earth is wrong with them?" Nori asked incredulously as she pointed to the nearest horse, a fat bay gelding with his forelock and mane standing straight up in rough spikes.

"Burrs," Justin said, laughing. "They must have found an old patch from last year in the pasture they were in. The seed pods are spikey and they stick to manes and tails like no tomorrow. It's not so bad picking them out if you know how, though. I use a handful of margarine to grease them up and then pick the burrs out one by one. It only takes a couple of hours."

I looked over at him to see if he was kidding but his face looked dead serious.

"Margarine? A couple of *hours* per horse?"

"Yep, does the trick every time. Although you might need two tubs for this lot."

"Well, I don't think we should clean them *all* up when we only need five," Nori said, "that would take forever."

"That's up to you guys. They're all well broke ranch horses. They were trained for packing beginners on the trail. But, like I said, they've been out of work over the winter and some might need more of a refresher than others. They've all been roped off at one point in their lives, but of course none of them have done horse archery. I'll put the first rides on anyone you pick out to make sure they're not hiding any tricks and then the rest will be up to you. Give me a shout once you've picked some out."

He sent us all a grin and headed back to the barn as fast as he could, probably sending up a prayer of thanks that this was not his mess to clean up.

We looked at the filthy horses grimly and they stared back, probably wondering what on earth we were doing.

"Well, maybe we should start by setting up a target outside the paddock and fire off some shots to see how they react," Rob said slowly, "that will give us a bit of an idea into their personalities anyway."

It was a good idea. Much better than trying to assess them all one by one to see which horses were naturally spooky and which ones were brave or interested in what we were doing. In the real world, of course, nearly any horse could be taught to be brave at archery with enough time and patience, but we had a pretty short timeline to work with so it would help if the horses we chose already had good natural instincts.

We'd left my old practice bow and our two foam targets in the broodmare barn tack room so it didn't take long to round up our supplies. Along with our archery stuff, we'd brought along a pile of faded, nylon halters and cotton lead ropes.

"All right," I said, arranging the target on an angle away from the horses so there wasn't any risk of an arrow bouncing back and hitting them, "I'll shoot, you guys assess. Any that look perfect, we'll put a halter on and take them to the broodmare barn to get cleaned up. After they settle in, we can do some groundwork with the archery stuff and we'll have Justin try them under saddle. We need five so how about we grab seven so we have a few spares."

"Sounds like a plan," Rob said.

He and Nori climbed the pipe-rail fence to study the little herd.

I drew an arrow from my quiver and without hesitating, I launched it at the target. The arrow hit with a loud *thunk*, and I felt a ripple run through the herd beside me. Someone snorted and on the other side of the paddock there was the sound of hooves striking the metal fence.

"Everything okay in there?"

"Yep," Rob said, "one of the chestnuts just got in a scuffle. Only a couple mildly spooked and most of the rest of them don't care. This little white one at the front is pretty interested. Shoot a few more."

I shot a grouping of five this time, one after another, pleased that they landed next to each other in a precise little bundle. I'd worked hard over the winter to improve my aim and accuracy, and it was satisfying to see all that work finally pay off.

There were a couple more snorts but over-all, they were a pretty relaxed bunch. I looked over to see a pale white horse with crazy blue eyes poking his nose through the bars, his upper lip wiggling.

"Oh, aren't you handsome. Do you want to see the bow?" I said laughing, since that seemed to be what he was looking at. "It's not edible you know."

I came over and tickled the end of his nose with my fingers and then let him sniff the bow, keeping an eye on those teeth. He was well behaved, though. He sniffed the bow from top to bottom as well as he could through the bars and then stuck out his tongue and began to lick the wood.

"Rob, he's just like Artimax," I said laughing, "Nori, put a halter on this one for sure."

Nori grabbed a handful of the nylon halters and climbed back over the fence into the paddock.

"Hey, buddy," she said moving up to scratch his shoulder. She made a face as she poked at the mass of burrs in his mane and forelock. "Oh my gosh, this is so gross. I can barely get his halter on."

"Well, do your best, he'll get cleaned up soon enough," Rob said. Then he pointed at a big red roan mare who looked half asleep. "That one, too. I like the look of her. Who else, Astrid?"

"Um," I surveyed the horses, trying to overlook their dirty coats and matted manes. They all looked pretty laid back. I had no idea how to pick out just seven. "Hang on."

I climbed the fence myself and then swung down the other side, landing in the paddock with a thump. Instantly, the little white horse came over to find me, nuzzling at my hands and then reaching down to check out my pockets. "Yes, yes. We already picked you. Now who else?"

I stared at the sea of horses looking mildly at me, scratching the white horse's neck with one hand while I tried to judge personalities in just one glance. The little horse suddenly lifted his nose and puffed a warm breath across my cheek, making me shiver.

A feeling of calm crept over me and for a second, it was just me in the center of this herd feeling safe and protected and sort of well, *connected.* Not just to the animals but to the ground and the sky, and to Rob and Nori, and to every living thing.

The feeling passed almost as fast as it came but the impression of connection lingered, and as I took a deep breath the horses nearest to me did, too.

"This bay," Nori said quietly, running her hand down the velvety nose of the round little mare that had sidled up to her. She glanced at us briefly for confirmation before buckling a halter over the mare's head.

The chestnut with the blaze looks nice, I thought, *he looks very wise.* It was funny how their expressions were all so different once you really took a few minutes to study them.

I went over to him, holding out my hand so he could sniff it and running a hand down his neck. He was also one of the few that wasn't completely matted with burrs so that was a bonus.

"Definitely this one."

"Just three more," Rob said.

In the end, we picked a black mare with a greying muzzle, a solid-looking buckskin gelding, and a black and white paint gelding with one brown eye and the other blue.

"Who knew that having a whole herd of horses to choose from would be so exhausting," Nori said.

"I know, that's like every horse person's dream." I said, laughing.

"Well, worst case scenario is that if one of them doesn't work out we just put it back and pick another one." Rob grinned and then his face became more serious. "We really shouldn't leave the rest of them all covered in burrs like that, though. It can't be comfortable."

"Are you kidding?" Nori looked at him incredulously. "It would take us years to clean them all up, and then they'd probably just be turned out back on that pasture and do it all over again. Maybe let's just focus on the seven we have."

Rob shrugged and jumped down off the fence, his face impassive. I groaned inwardly. Rob was not the type of guy to back away from hard work and I had the feeling that, at some point in the near future, I was about to get dragged into the clean-up project of a lifetime.

CHAPTER 9

It took us a while to ferry the first group of our chosen horses all the way over to the broodmare barn, and then we realized that we hadn't planned ahead enough to actually have stalls ready for them. We had to throw them together in the small paddock out front while we located the straw, bedded down the stalls, set up water buckets, and shook out flakes of hay for everyone.

The morning breeze had disappeared and we were all hot and sweaty by the time everyone was transferred over and finally settled into their new homes.

I was exhausted and we'd barely even gotten started.

"Do you know these horses, Red? Were some of these your friends?" He'd stuck his head far over his stall door to see his neighbour, the wise-looking chestnut gelding, his eyes wide with excitement. Nothing much fazed him and he was used to all sorts of horses coming and going, so I was surprised at how interested he was in the new arrivals. For all I knew, the chestnut was his brother or something. They had the same kind expressions and the same thin, silky manes. Which was lucky for me because I'd already used my fingers to strip out half of the burrs that were clinging to the chestnut's mane and forelock. He was going to be an easy project, unlike the little white horse, whose mane, tail, and forelock were packed so solidly with burrs that he looked like a spiky unicorn.

"I guess we'll have to find out what their names are and make some signs for their doors," Nori said from a few stalls down. "I don't want to be calling this one the little bay mare for the next month."

It had been easy enough to divide them up between us. Rob didn't mind which ones he worked with anyway and Nori had claimed the bay and the paint as her own right away, and I'd known from the start that I wanted the white gelding and the chestnut.

"Well, I guess I'll take the roan and the black mare," Rob said, laughing. I knew that he honestly didn't care since he rode lots of client horses back home and new horses weren't quite the novelty for him that they were for us. "The buckskin will just have to be a group project. At least until we figure out which ones will work best for the clinic."

"I hope this isn't going to be too much work for you guys," I said, wincing. "We still have our own horses to ride and Lillian wants you to pick out your young project horses, too."

"Oh, stop worrying," Nori said, waving her hand through the air. "Riding is what we're here to do, right? Besides, Mara told me that she can help us too, if we get stuck."

"Yeah, that's a good idea actually," I said, remembering that Liza had asked me to include Mara whenever we could. "I'm not sure when she'll be able to get away, though. She has a pretty full work load here already."

"I don't know," Nori said with a shrug. "But she told me that she didn't mind helping out with the clinic when we need her. She's a good rider and you said she's good at archery."

"Better than good, she's great. She was one of the best on our school archery team."

"Come on, I'm starving," Rob broke in. "Let's go have lunch and we'll start cleaning these guys up afterward."

"Yeah, I don't think I can face this project without food, either," I said and we headed tiredly up to the house.

CHAPTER 10

Allan had left by the time we got back and Aunt Lillian looked a little subdued as she set out the ingredients for our ham sandwiches and potato salad. I'd always found her cooking a little hit and miss when I'd lived at the ranch; either she was creating gigantic feasts fit for an army or she was shoving a box a crackers and a block of cheese into my hands and telling me to fend for myself. I hadn't minded at all, of course. At the time I'd just been glad someone was feeding me. But it was a little disconcerting sometimes not to know what to expect.

The front door banged open, and boots and voices sounded in the hallway as everyone trooped inside.

It was ranch tradition that everyone who worked there came up to the house to eat breakfast and lunch if they could. It was a time to discuss the livestock, chores, and endless repairs. They came in smelling like hay, sweat, sunshine and horses.

Mara had a streak of dirt across her forehead and Casey had bits of hay twisted in her pony-tail.

"Dad had me re-organizing the hay room." She sighed heavily as I quickly picked the greenery out of her hair and threw them in the garbage bin. "That was after I cleaned out practically all the stalls in the training barn. I'm so glad I start summer-school tomorrow."

"Um, you'll still have chores to do," her dad said, laying a hand firmly on her shoulder, "that was our deal."

"Yeah, yeah, but not so many. And I have to concentrate on all that extra school work so I can become a rich genius who supports your horse habit."

Bryce raised his eyebrows and shook his head but he was smiling. Despite how bossy Casey could be, I knew that her dad was proud of how smart she was and that she had goals that didn't involve the ranch. Everyone else in her family was completely horse-centered, but Casey had forged out her own path and I knew Bryce respected her for that.

"I can't see why anyone would volunteer to go to school in the summer," Mara grumbled.

"I didn't volunteer. I saved up and paid to go," Casey said defensively.

"That's even worse." Mara laughed.

Casey opened her mouth to say something but Aunt Lillian cut her off.

"No arguing at the table, ladies. You know the rules. Get your food and sit down. We have lots to discuss and the day's not getting any younger."

They both shut up after that and there was just the sound of scraping chairs as everyone found a seat and then a long silence while everyone gratefully shovelled in the food in front of them.

"Right, well, did you kids pick out some horses?"

"Yes," I said, since she was looking at me. "They're in the broodmare barn already. We just have to clean them up still. We picked seven just in case we needed extras or someone went lame or something. They'll need their feet done, too."

"Right. That's on my list. That whole group of ranch horses needs to get spruced up, actually. It wouldn't hurt if any of the people at the clinic were impressed enough to want to buy a horse or two. We can offer a good rate."

"What? Like you mean they're all for sale?" Nori asked, her eyes widening.

"Well, they don't have much of a purpose here at this point. We're not doing trail rides anymore and we already have enough horses in our lesson string to get along. Most of those horses are just sitting idle. It would be nice to clean them up and get some eyes on them. There's a ranch horse auction coming up in the fall, but I'd rather not send them there unless I have to."

"But don't horses get sold for *meat* at auctions?" Nori said incredulously.

Everyone stopped eating and turned to look at her, surprised at her outburst.

Nori wilted a little under all that scrutiny but she kept her gaze fixed firmly on Aunt Lillian.

"Ah, not at the higher priced auctions," my aunt said quickly. "Not usually. There are auctions that are specifically for working stock, and people only go there to find good riding and working horses. You can even set a minimum bid so that they're over meat prices."

Nori nodded but she didn't look exactly convinced.

I thought of our seven project horses and then of all the other ungroomed, burr-laden horses we'd left behind in the paddock. That was a lot of horses to try and find homes for. Plus the young horses that she was hoping Rob would take on for her. It was probably optimistic to think that all of them would find good riding homes. What would happen to the ones that didn't?

"How were the morning lessons, Liza?" my aunt said, changing the subject abruptly.

"Good, as always. One of the girls wants to bring her horse here for a month of training and lessons. I said I'd see when we could free up a spot in the barn."

"We can free up a spot," Bryce said, between bites of sandwich. "Any cash flow is good so tell her to come on over. It might be a little chaotic during the tournament thing but the more the merrier, I say. Those two yearlings will be gone at the end of the month, too."

As I listened I was reminded all over again about what it took to run a place like this. Bryce, Justin, and Liza all trained Aunt Lillian's sale and show horses and took in outside sales and training horses as well. Justin and Liza both taught lessons, and then there were the young stock to work with, too. Plus, the band of broodmares and the flocks of sheep that had to be kept fed and healthy.

I really didn't know how they got everything done in a day.

I drifted off in my own thoughts for a while, wondering if this was the sort of life I'd want for myself. I definitely knew I wanted to have horses in my life forever. But a big operation like this where there was hardly a moment for yourself? I didn't know. It was certainly much better than the life I'd had growing up in my sterile condo in the city where nobody laughed or got muddy or came home with hay in their hair.

"Hey, are you done eating?" Rob asked, bumping his shoulder gently against mine. I shook my head to find that everyone else had finished and were getting up to put their plates in the dishwasher. I'd missed the whole rest of the conversation.

"Um, almost," I said, wolfing down the rest of my sandwich and wondering what I'd missed.

I think I was still sleepy from our sixteen-hour trip the day before because with the lunch sitting freshly in my stomach and the sun high overhead, all I wanted to do was have a long afternoon nap.

It seemed an effort to walk to the truck and drive down to the barn. Even Nori was uncharacteristically silent in the back seat so I was pretty sure that everyone felt the same way.

It turned out that after lunch was siesta time for the horses, too. When we reached the barn, we found that only a few of them were inside. All the rest had gone out to the back of their paddocks and were stretched out full-length in the sunshine. Including Red and the sheep.

I took one look at them and burst out laughing because Portia was flat out and Red had somehow managed to position himself so he could use her pudgy belly as a pillow for his head. I could even hear him snoring gently.

"You don't see that every day," Rob said, shaking his head. "You sure have some weird pets, Astrid."

"Yeah." I couldn't even deny it. "They're the best."

"I wish I had my phone so I could take a picture for Callie," Nori said laughing. "She'd love this for her sheep photo collection."

"What, you don't have it on you? I thought that thing was practically surgically attached to you."

"No, there's no point without any internet." She broke off and looked away abruptly. "And honestly, I'm glad to have a break from it. Not a single person can get a hold of me no matter what. It's like being released from prison."

I thought that was a little dramatic but she was already walking back into the barn, whistling a little tune under her breath.

I took a few pictures to send to Callie later. There was free Wi-Fi in town and I knew we'd probably go in a few days so we could catch up with what was happening in the outside world.

It seemed heartless to wake the sleeping horses up from their naps so I went back into the barn and walked down the aisle to see who was still inside. Maybe I could get started on cleaning someone up.

"Oh, you're in here, are you?" I said as a white nose poked out over one of the stall doors. "Would you like some attention?"

He bobbed his nose up and down, and I had the feeling that he was the sort of guy who would *always* want attention.

"I think it's going to be easier to do this without your halter on," I told him. I had a habit of talking to the horses like they were people, and although some of the boarders at our barn at home gave me strange looks, I'd never seen a reason to give it up. Sometimes the horses even seemed to understand what I was saying, although other times I think they just tuned me out.

I went down to the hay room and grabbed a flake for him, stopping at the tack room on the way back for my grooming tote.

"Hey, since my horses are all passed out, do you mind if I go watch Mara ride?" Nori asked. "Liza's helping her with that chestnut horse and her lesson should be starting any second. I could come back right afterward."

"Oh, sure," I said, "just.—"

I broke off, biting back the words I'd been about to say, *don't get in the way, don't bother anyone, don't get hurt...* all things her mother might say. But she didn't need to hear any of that from me.

"Just have fun," I finished lamely.

"Yeah, okay, bye."

I sighed and looked up to find Rob laughing at me. "I don't know why you're laughing," I said, smiling despite myself. "You know this means we'll most likely have to de-burr her horses, too. She'll probably show up the second we're done."

"Most likely." He nodded and headed into the roan mare's stall with his own flake of hay.

"All right, horse," I said to the little white gelding, "I don't have a tub of margarine but I do have Show-sheen and detangler so one of those will just have to do the trick."

He happily worked away at his hay pile while I tackled his mane from bottom to top. It was quite something. The prickly little burrs were about the size of a quarter and were shaped like perfect spiky spheres that caught the hair and wrapped it around in tight circles until the whole mane was twisted into one solid matt. It was hard to know exactly where to start so I just sprayed the entire mane with Show-sheen and used my mane comb to pick one hair free at a time.

The white horse didn't seem to care too much, only swishing his equally matted tail now and then when I accidentally pulled too hard.

"Sorry," I said, scratching his neck in apology. "I'm being as careful as I can."

At first I'd just been pulling out the burrs and dropping them, and it wasn't until I happened to glance down that I saw that the fallen spiky seed pods were already clinging to his legs and his chin hair. If I went on like that he'd be fully covered from the feet up in no time.

"This is the worst plant on the planet," I said out loud, scooping up all the fallen ones I could see and tossing them into the aisle.

Gradually, piece by piece, his snowy white mane came free. It was all frizzy underneath; like hair that had been left in braids too long. But the strands were thick and lustrous, and I was sure that it was going to be beautiful once I was done.

Rob's horse was in the stall next to mine and we plucked away in companionable silence, lost in our work, comfortable enough with each other that we didn't even need to say anything. The only sounds were the horses crunching, the occasional ting of a mane comb and the satisfying whisper of burrs falling steadily to the aisle floor.

It took me nearly two hours to finish that horse from top to bottom and by the end, my fingers were pricked and stinging, and I had worn two raw grooves into my index fingers from pulling endless strands. The white horse's body had been groomed to a luminous shine, and his mane and tail fell in waves against his coat.

"I can't believe we're actually finished," I said, staring at him in satisfaction. "Now you can never, ever go near one of those burr bushes again. They should all be burned to the ground on sight."

He sent me a bit of a grumpy look as he rooted around for the last few bits of hay. He was a nice horse but even his patience had been running thin by the end. Although you'd think a little pulling would still feel nicer than ten pounds of spiky burrs poking his skin.

"Hey, Rob, this guy is really well put together," I said, leaning back against the stall to survey my handiwork. "It's hard to believe he's an old seasoned ranch horse. He looks pretty young."

"That's what I was kind of thinking, too," Rob said, coming out of the mares stall with a handful of burrs in one hand. He dropped them on top of our giant pile and stretched his arms backward, making a face as he worked the kinks out of his muscles.

"Can't you tell his age by looking at his teeth or something?"

"Technically, yes, but I actually have no idea how to do that."

"Oooh," I said teasingly. "I thought you knew absolutely *every*thing about horses. I thought you were perfect."

"Close," he said, reaching up swiftly to tickle me in that sensitive spot behind my ear. Some people are ticklish on their ribs or behind their knees, but for me it was the side of my neck, and I squealed and ducked away, making him laugh, and the white horse toss up his head.

"Sorry, horse," I said quickly, still laughing.

"Well, my hands are killing me," Rob said, "we should take a break."

"Definitely. I was thinking that we should take pictures of all these guys to show Justin. That way he can at least give us all their names and details. I don't want to be calling this guy little white horse forever."

"He's actually not that little. And I could be totally wrong here but I think he has some more growing to do, too."

"Maybe he was started under saddle really early."

"Probably. These horses are so mellow that you can hardly tell the difference between an old trail horse and a young one. They're practically born trained."

"Aunt Lillian says that's mostly genetics with a sprinkle of good handling and training."

"She should know, I guess. She's been breeding for a long time and she sure produces enough of them."

I glanced at him quickly but his face was impassive. Rob was the ultimate horse professional who would never say a critical thing about anyone except as a last resort. Getting an opinion out of him sometimes was like pulling teeth.

I used my phone to take a couple of shots of the two horses we'd cleaned up and grabbed some apples out of my backpack for our snacks.

The sun was beating down on us but it seemed more of an effort to get into the un-air-conditioned truck and drive over to the training barn than it did to just walk down.

We stayed near the edge of the rutted trail where the towering trees threw at least a little shade and walked side by side, linking our pinky fingers like we sometimes did when we were on our own. Such a little link but powerful too in its own way.

I didn't believe in things like soul mates or love at first sight or anything, but I had to admit that Rob made me a better person. I always felt smarter, braver and stronger when he was around. I didn't know if that was his essential *goodness* rubbing off on me or if his presence just brought my best traits to the surface. All I knew was that when he was beside me I felt sort of invincible.

The training barn was so nice and cool after the afternoon heat that we both let out audible sighs of relief when we walked inside and then started laughing.

"We're really going to have to toughen up if we're going to survive a month of this," Rob said, "we're not on the island anymore."

"Oh, I know. The swarms of killer mosquitos that tried to assassinate us last night were my first clue."

The barn was quiet. Most of the horses were still inside dozing and we went quietly down the aisle to look for Justin.

We found him cantering a grey gelding in circles in the arena and Liza was cooling out the sweaty chestnut stallion, Fox, on a loose rein.

"Oh, my gosh, Astrid," Nori said, looking up guiltily from her spot on the bleachers. "I'm so sorry, I totally lost track of time. I've just been watching these guys work. They're both amazing."

"Oh, it's fine," I said, "your horses will still be waiting for you when you get back. I've learnt that burrs are evil, though. It's a completely pointless plant."

"Hey," Liza called, nudging Fox in our direction. "How is your beautification project coming?"

"Er, slow. And a little painful." I held up my reddened hands for her to see.

"Yikes. Yeah, they're something else, aren't they? We'll need to figure out some time for lessons for you as a reward."

"That would be amazing. I wouldn't mind riding Quarry again if he's sound. I miss that."

She made a face and shook her head. "Sorry, kiddo, he's fully retired now and he loves it. We can ride out to visit him after dinner if you like. He and Marcus are down by the lake with the broodmare band right now. Marcus worked hard all winter so I turned him out for a month of vacation. He's coming along really nicely, though."

I nodded, trying to look pleased for Quarry. Of course I was happy that he was enjoying his well-deserved retirement, but a small part of me had hoped that he'd be sound enough to ride, even a little bit, so I could experience that magic just one more time.

Quarry had been the first horse I'd had lessons on and I hadn't understood at the time what a privilege it had been to ride him. I'd been a complete beginner and hadn't known that not all horses could spontaneously elevate into a perfect piaffe and passage when they were feeling a little fancy. And that the subtle seat, leg, and breathing aids that Claudia had taught me were not something that every instructor even knew how to teach.

It's funny how we don't appreciate the good things we have until much later sometimes, I thought with a sigh as we followed Liza and Fox from the ring. I still loved riding but I missed those early days when everything was brand new and shining. Quarry had been more like a magical creature to me than a real horse, and he'd been a wise and generous teacher just as much as Claudia had been. Red was my best friend but lately Oona and I'd been the one teaching *him* to do things. Or maybe it was more accurate to say that we'd been learning how to do things together.

I guess that's part of growing as a rider though, I thought a little wistfully, *first you are a beginner, then a student and finally, you become a teacher yourself.*

CHAPTER 11

We helped cool out Fox and give him a bath while Mara swiftly appeared to tack up Liza and Justin's next horses. It was a treat to watch both of them ride. They had different styles but each of them looked like they'd merged with their horses completely, their aids were mostly invisible and the horses moved in an effortless, happy way like they were totally in tune with their riders.

"We'd better get back," Rob said with a sigh, as reluctant as I was to leave. We'd watched two more sets of horses already though, and time was ticking away. "We have our own horses waiting. Come on Nori, you too."

The air outside was scorching, a sharp contrast after being in the cool barn for hours. We hurried up the trail as fast as we could, clinging to the last remaining bits of shade that dotted the dusty road. When we got there we found Casey sitting cross-legged in the aisle with a book in front of her and three giant tubs of margarine stacked off to one side.

"Finally," she said. "I thought you'd never get here. "Dad sent me to give this to you. You guys are working way harder than you need to. Margarine is like miracle sauce when you're dealing with burrs."

She laughed when she saw our skeptical faces. "Don't believe me? Just watch."

The paint horse was standing inside with his head leaning over his stall door, his eyes half-closed and his lower lip drooping as he napped. He didn't even have time to react before Casey had pried open the lid to one of the tubs, scooped out a giant handful of yellow goo, walked over and splatted it right on the horse's matted forelock.

"Whoa," she said sharply, as the horse opened his eyes wide and tried to pull away. He stopped instantly, only reacting again when she reached over the stall and slopped more of the goop across his mane, working it in with her fingers. He looked like he was a cake being covered in frosting.

"Just give it a sec to absorb in," she said, giving the horse a sticky pat on the neck. "Right, which one is next?"

We reluctantly opened all the tubs and followed her lead. Slathering each horse one by one until they were all slathered with a thick layer of yellow.

Casey looked on with satisfaction as Rob, Nori, and I started combing the greasy burrs out of the first couple of horses and the sharp little seed pods began to rain to the aisle floor.

"It's like magic," I said, as the burrs slid free.

"It's disgusting," Nori complained. "They'll be so gross and greasy afterwards."

"They'll just be moisturized," Casey said. "You can always give them a bath when you're done. You're welcome, by the way."

Despite the mess and the grease, it was totally worth it and I think we all breathed a collective sigh of relief when it was finally over. Even the horses seemed much happier.

"My Dad said you could bring a few of them over to the training barn as soon as you're ready," Casey said. "He told Justin to find some tack for them and maybe put a ride on them if he has a second."

"And hopefully tell us what their names are," Nori said, leading her paint horse out into the aisle toward the wash rack.

"Um, I think that's Whiskey," Casey said, looking thoughtfully at the paint. "And that roan mare Rob has is definitely Kestrel, that's Kitty's half-sister, and Astrid your chestnut.... Um, I think that's related to Fox somehow. Firefly? Fizzle? I can't remember, we'll have to ask my dad or Justin."

"Sorry, buddy, you'll have to stay nameless for now," I whispered to him, running my hand down his neck. He snorted, still half-asleep, not caring what I called him. "Would you like a bath, too?"

He wasn't covered in quite as much margarine as the others since only his tail had needed doing but he still hadn't been groomed in ages and his coat was dull with dust and dirt. It wouldn't hurt to get him clean too, and the horses would dry quickly in the heat.

All the horses stood perfectly for their baths, proof of their good natures and that they'd been handled quite a bit in the past.

"Did you ever have your own person, buddy?" I asked the chestnut, stripping the water from his coppery coat. "Were you always a guest horse or did you have someone special to fuss over you at one time?"

He blinked at me and nudged my arm softly, not giving away any secrets.

When our first three horses were clean, we let them amble toward the training barn, walking slowly and stopping to let them graze from time to time to give their coats a chance to dry properly. The sun was now in definite scorch mode and my tee shirt was already sticking to my back even though I'd made sure to turn some of the spray from the hose on myself to cool down. This was one thing I certainly hadn't missed about living here.

The ocean breezes back home kept the heat of summer relatively tolerable.

Coming into the training barn again was a hard relief, and I remembered again why desperate people paid hundreds of thousands of dollars to build themselves indoor arenas that were safe from the elements.

"Hello again, everyone," Justin called, poking his head out of the tack room. "Just throw them in cross-ties and we'll find some gear that fits them. We only have a million saddles in here to choose from."

I clipped the chestnut to the wall then went to the tack room doorway and stopped, putting my hands on my hips in mock outrage. "What have you guys done to my nice, clean tack room?" I said because putting their dirty, chaotic tack room into order had been one of my projects back when I'd lived here. I'd cleaned and organized it until it was sparkling. And I bet it hadn't taken them any time at all to let it revert into chaos.

Saddles were piled one on top of the other, sometimes stacked three high. A few bridles hung on the wall but the majority of them were heaped in a huge dirty pile on the floor next to the sink.

"Liza's section is clean," Justin said, winking, pointing to the corner near the door where a handful of dressage saddles hung neatly on their racks. There was a deep wall-unit where a saddle-pad collection, organized by colour, sat next to rows and rows of multi-coloured polo wraps. The bridles were all cleaned, oiled, and hung up in a precise row with their throat-latches done up in figure-eights to contain them in identical bundles.

"Ah, now that's more like it," I said approvingly.

"Sorry, Astrid, we don't have much time for the fancy stuff around here. But, I won't say no if you'd like to get this space cleaned up again. We sure missed how tidy everything was when you were here."

He grinned at me and I narrowed my eyes, knowing a sucker-move when I saw it.

"Uh-huh, I'll bet." I sighed, mentally adding the tack room to the growing list of things that needed help on the ranch.

"Um, okay, grab a few bridles from that pile and I'll bring the saddles. Let's see what these old horses have to say."

If I'd had any doubts that using ranch horses that had had an entire season off was a good idea, they were quickly laid to rest when I watched Justin work with them in the ring. He free-lunged each one briefly first and then hopped up on them one at a time. They didn't miss a beat and acted like they'd never even had an extended vacation at all. They weren't fancy but they walked, trotted, and cantered obediently in each direction without any fuss, did a few steps of basic leg yielding and some quarter turns.

"These horses are bred to work," Justin said, "and that's what they like to do. These guys will be fine for you to play around with. But they're all out of shape so you need to start them off slow so that they don't get sore or sour, right? Just light work and trail riding for a few days before you do much in the ring. I have to get back to work but bring the rest of them over tomorrow afternoon for me to look at."

"You're a good boy," I told the chestnut, whose name had turned out to be *Fenwick* of all things. "Maybe someone at this clinic will see how handsome you are and take you home with them. Would you like that?"

CHAPTER 12

Dinner was another noisy affair with everyone on the ranch crowded around the big table, talking over each other. I was too tired to say much. Part of me longed to just crawl upstairs to bed but Liza had invited us on a trail ride to see Quarry and Marcus with the broodmare band that night and there was no way I was missing out on that.

Foaling season had been intense when I'd lived here and I had spent many late nights on foal watch. There had been so many amazing moments and one horrible, awful night when Red's elderly mom Beezy had died. Her foal Figaro had been the one Folly had taken under her wing. We'd still had to bottle feed him of course, but she'd taken on the role of being his surrogate mom.

I'd had some idea of Rob and I slipping away on our own to have a peaceful trail ride with Liza and Justin but my plans went off the rails the second Nori overheard.

"We're going on another trail ride?" she said excitedly. "I mean Maverick's already been out today but maybe I can take one of the ranch horses if the ride isn't too hard. Justin, could I take the paint? I mean Whiskey? He would be okay, wouldn't he?"

"Umm, yeah, probably," Justin said, breaking away from his

conversation with his dad to answer her. "It's an easy enough ride."

"Great, and could Mara and Casey come, too? Rob and Astrid have their own horses, so that way Fenwick and Kestrel could get ridden, too."

"Who?" Aunt Lillian asked, looking confused.

"The ranch horses," Nori said, frowning. "Those are their names."

"Oh, right. I lose track of those ones. They all blend together after a while."

Luckily, she was looking back down at her dinner so she missed the dark look Nori sent her.

"Well Salsa and I are going, too," Olive said firmly from her end of the table. "We're not being left behind."

In the end, everyone but Aunt Lillian and the sheep came, and it turned out to be almost as fun as if we'd snuck away on our own. Everyone was in high spirits. The horses perked up in the cooler evening air and got a little spring in their steps.

Red marched along underneath me, his nose bobbing happily and his ears pricked as he stared around his old home with interest. So far he seemed to be enjoying his vacation quite a bit.

The air had cooled down to a bearable level and as we climbed higher into the hills the temperature dropped steadily and a light breeze skittered across my arms.

"This is the scenic route," I told Rob. "You can get down to the lake by going the other way too, but it's not nearly so pretty."

We wound our way through a small scrubby forest and then came out on the lower ridge that overlooked the valley and the lake below.

There were higher ridges above us where the views were even more spectacular, but this was pretty stunning. The lake spread out below us, a round body with outstretched arms like a starfish that reached into the low, rolling hills surrounding it. Even from here I could see the horses dotting the pasture around it and I even thought I might be able to make out Quarry's snowy coat.

The downward path curved gently through the slope, weaving back and forth so neatly that it hardly felt like you were going downhill at all. The horses moved at an easy pace, hips swaying and heads bobbing to their own rhythms.

"Do you think those guys are up for a short canter?" Justin asked when we reached the flatter ground below. He glanced over at Mara.

She patted Fenwick's neck and reached down to feel his chest which was cool and dry.

"Sure, I think so," she said, glancing at Nori and Casey. And when both girls nodded she signaled the chestnut to move into a canter. Red was eager to follow and leapt forward when I asked him, his ears pricked and his neatly pulled mane tossing in the breeze.

This must be what being part of a galloping herd feels like, I thought, caught up in the synchronized rumble of so many hooves hitting the ground at once. I'd gone on hundreds of trail rides but never with so many people, and never on a wide open plain where we could just fly along side by side. It was magical.

A dirt road appeared and then a fence, and we slowed to a trot and then a walk, the horses puffing and snorting with pride and excitement.

Bryce sidled his horse up to the gate, leaned down to unlatch it and did a perfect side-pass so the gate swung open for the rest of us. And then he swivelled his horse around and closed it the same way. It didn't even look like he'd given the animal any signal to move at all but the horse performed perfectly.

The pasture sloped gently downward and suddenly there was the lake, the blue waters turned a mixture of dark purple and pink with the setting sun. And there were the horses. The mares, round-bellied and bony-hipped, barely glancing at us as they were so intent on eating the long grass. Most of them were older, seasoned mares who were used to horses, trucks and quads coming and going so nothing much excited them.

The foals were thrilled at the company though, they whinnied shrilly and flagged their fluffy little tails in the air, tossing their heads and prancing toward us. Getting as close as they dared before whirling around and racing back toward their mothers.

I watched them in awe, marveling at how perfectly adorable they were with their slender legs lifting in lofty trots that carried them across the grass like they had wings.

From the far edge of the herd, Quarry and Marcus appeared, marching steadily toward us. Quarry looked mildly interested but Marcus let out a bugling neigh that shook his whole body.

"Calm down you goof," Liza called affectionately. She jumped down off the buckskin mare she was riding and handed the reins to Justin before going forward to plant herself between Marcus and the riders.

"You just calm down and behave yourself," she said, fishing around in her pocket until she found a cookie for him. He crunched it appreciatively then swung his head around to nicker at Quarry who came ambling up beside him.

"Can you hold Red for me?" I asked Rob. It was hardly necessary since Red had already found a lush patch of grass and was steadily working on it.

My heart thumped a few extra beats when I saw Quarry watching me.

"Hey, buddy," I said, approaching him slowly. He pricked his ears and nickered a little under his breath. I wasn't sure if it was because he remembered me or if he just thought I might have a treat for him, but I felt a glow of happiness anyway as we approached each other. I let him sniff my hand for a second in greeting and then I moved forward and wrapped his strong, white neck in a tight hug.

His coat was smooth and warm, and I inhaled deeply as a whole summer's worth of memories swept over me.

"Thanks, friend," I told him, drawing back and smoothing out his silky mane. He snorted and then dropped his head to graze nearby, one ear turned in our direction.

Everyone else had jumped down to stretch their legs and admire the broodmare band and the foals. There was a big discussion going on about which mare was which and who was the mother of which of the two- and three-year-olds in training.

"Are they all bred again for this year?" I asked and there was a sudden silence.

"Ah, no," Bryce said finally. "We decided to give most of them a season off to recover. Some of them are older and could use a break. And that gives us some time to catch up on some things around the ranch. We'll have a couple foals next year but not many."

I nodded but secretly wondered what Aunt Lillian had thought of that plan. The broodmare herd was her responsibility and I knew she loved taking care of the mares and foals.

We stayed out as long as we could, until the pink sky darkened and the bugs descended on us in a swarm. There was no taking the scenic route this time. We moved at a brisk trot, taking the direct short cut that led to the big barn.

We said a hasty goodnight to Liza, Justin, and Bryce, and the rest of us trotted up to the broodmare barn and got safely inside before the mosquitos ate us alive.

Red and Artimax were barely breathing hard; they were used to being ridden on our hilly, sandy trails almost every day. But the ranch horses looked a little tired as they gratefully tucked into their hay.

"I hope we didn't do too much with them," I said, looking at Fenwick's half-closed eyes. There was a dark square of sweat on his back where the saddle blanket had been and his haunches quivered a little as Casey ran the curry comb across them in circles.

"Naw, they'll be fine.," she said, giving him a pat. "It's always a bit hard for them when they first start back into work but they know the routine. They'll be back in shape in a few weeks' time."

Luckily for all of us, Bryce arrived with the truck so we didn't have to walk home.

"Make sure you put on some bug spray tomorrow," he warned. "Your aunt has cans of it stashed everywhere. You'll get eaten right up if you don't spray some on a few times a day."

"Oh, I don't believe in using toxic poisons on my skin," Nori said, raising her eyebrows at him like he'd suggested she leap off a cliff.

"Aww, that's cute. That's what most city people say when they first get here," Bryce said, laughing under his breath. "You'll learn soon enough."

CHAPTER 13

As much as I agreed with Nori about not wanting to slather myself in chemicals, the mosquito swarms wore me down the next morning. A big cloud of them were right by the front door waiting for me when I opened it. I shut it firmly again and went for the bug spray.

When I went outside again, I could practically see the swarm parting in disappointment, driven back by the horrible smell of citronella, pine, and chemicals now clinging to me.

"Ha, take that," I told them as I marched toward the truck. Rob had already gone down to the barn ahead of me to feed since it was my morning to sleep in an extra half-hour, and our plan was to work with the horses and clean paddocks together while it was still cool out.

Nori had headed out on another early morning trail ride since it was the only time either Casey or Mara could get away. Casey's summer classes at the local private school started after ten o' clock and went all day, so this was the only time she had to ride and Mara would have her hands full with work until sunset.

"Don't work with the bay mare without me," Nori had begged

and we'd agreed that we'd leave her until last. We'd have plenty of work to do anyway.

Both Justin and Liza had a full day of lessons going on so Rob and I had decided to use the little pen outside the broodmare barn to test out our next group of ranch horses ourselves. The last group had been so well behaved that we were fairly confident that this group would be okay, too.

Rob picked the black mare to bring out first since she looked about twenty years old and had a very sweet, calm expression. We brushed her together and then Rob led her to the makeshift ring we'd made up in the paddock and free-lunged her at a walk and then a trot. It was really too small for loping but he asked her for a few steps just to make sure she was able to pick up the canter at all and then he just worked with her on the ground, asking her to lead politely beside him, to stop and back up and swing her quarters away when he asked. She was sweet and polite the entire time so we felt pretty comfortable tacking her up.

I held her reins while Rob swung aboard but it wasn't needed at all. She gazed at me with a mild expression and then moved around the pen when he asked, picking up all gaits without hesitation.

"She'll be perfect for one of our beginner riders," Rob said, patting her fondly. "We should do some shooting beside her today before we put her away. She's way further ahead than I thought she'd be."

I hurried to drag out our target from the tack room and set it up outside the pen.

Rob had already jumped off and I handed him his bow and a quiver full of arrows.

I held her reins just in case while he shot, and then stepped away when she didn't even flinch. He shot a few more arrows and then mounted up to shoot a few off her back while I held her reins again.

The mare opened her mouth in a deep yawn as the arrows sailed through the air and hit the target with solid *thunking* sounds. She blinked sleepily and then closed her eyes, her lower lip drooping.

She was doing so well that I even led her around at a walk so Rob could practice shooting while she was moving. She honestly could not care less what we did.

"Well, that could not have gone better," I said laughing as Rob jumped to the ground, "you are such a perfect girl. I can't wait to have a name to call you by."

"All right, I'll get her untacked and put away if you want to pick the next one."

"The white gelding," I said instantly, because I'd been dying to work with him from the first moment I saw him. "I'll brush him and meet you in the ring."

"Okay." Rob led the mare over to the wash rack to give her a proper bath, and I saw her close her eyes in pleasure as the first light spray of water misted over her back.

"All right, little guy," I told my friend who was already standing with his head over the door and his ears pricked as if he'd already guessed that he was to be next.

He was much different than the mare, though. He stood politely enough while I brushed him but he was not asleep. He kept his head up and his ears pricked, peering over the stall door so he could watch the water from the hose spraying outside. He shifted his weight obediently when I picked up his feet, but he sighed a few times and pressed his chest against the door as if he was ready to be done with brushing. We wanted to get out and do something less boring.

We hadn't fitted him out with his own saddle yet so I just grabbed the one Fenwick had used the day before, hoping that it would be a good enough fit for just a short, initial ride.

I brushed the saddle pad off as best I could and laid it carefully over his back, watching his expression. When he didn't react, I went for the saddle. He certainly didn't mind being tacked up but was interested in the saddle and turned around to lip at the stirrups, investigating them one by one. His head popped up a little when I did up his cinch, but he relaxed again right away.

When I led him out of the stall, he strode after me, each foot coming down solidly on the dirt floor. No dragging toes or sluggish steps, he moved with a purposeful stride that was full of energy. I had the feeling that, as affectionate as he was, he would not be a beginner's horse.

"All right, little white, let's see you do a bit of lunging." I let him go and shook the lead rope a little to move him away from me. Again, he was polite; he kept one ear locked on me as he walked and trotted around the little ring. There was no bucking or kicking, but his trot was definitely more animated than the other horses had been and he didn't seem as balanced. His head popped up every few strides and then it dropped down again.

He's just younger, I guess, I thought, admiring the curve of his neck and the way he bent his hocks as he propelled himself forward.

"He's definitely flashier than the others," Rob said, frowning thoughtfully as we brought the horse in to the center of the pen and I fitted him with the bridle. "How has he been acting for you?"

"Perfectly well-behaved," I said honestly. "But he definitely doesn't seem as experienced as the others. He's taking everything in stride, but I wonder how much training he really has on board."

"You want me to get on him first?" Rob asked but I shook my head. I wasn't usually the bravest when it came to riding strange horses, but there was something about this horse that made me trust him. And for whatever reason I wanted to be the one to ride him first.

I almost regretted it though once I was on board. He stood perfectly still when I mounted but once he began walking, his way of going was much different than Red's. Red was powerful but calm and slow, with long, smooth strides. This gelding had a big stride too, but it was quick and the tempo was uneven. It was like he'd rush a bit with his front end and the back end would have to catch up. And in the corners he didn't bend with his body in an arc so much as pivot on his hind end in a sort of jerky, stiff movement.

I was very uncomfortable for the first few minutes until I realized that he didn't mean any harm. The weird, rushy steps were just the way he moved and not a sign that he was about to buck or scoot out from underneath me. It was like he was trying to keep himself balanced underneath my weight.

And it got better the longer we walked, the tension drained away and he let out a huge sigh and dropped his head.

"See what he's like going the other direction," Rob said quietly. He'd climbed the fence and was sitting on the top rail with his legs dangling inside the ring.

I asked him to switch directions but instead of letting me guide him in a half-circle, he bulged against my leg and drifted to the outside. It was almost like he didn't know he was supposed to be turning.

"What are you doing, little guy?" I asked him, giving his neck a scratch. I turned him back in the opposite direction but this time I steered him like I would a baby horse, gently opening my inside rein way out to the side so he could make the turn. This time he followed my lead perfectly and I was now pretty sure what the problem was. I walked a few more circles and changed direction a couple more times, noticing that he was improving and gaining confidence the more laps we rode.

"Hey, Rob," I said, easing the gelding to a gentle stop and giving him a good scratch on the neck. "I don't know how this guy got in with the group, but I don't think he's a seasoned ranch horse at all."

"I agree." He laughed. "I bet he's only had a couple rides on him at all. If that."

"He's great, though. I wish we could keep working with him." I looked down at the gelding's neck and sighed. It was silly, really, but as soon as I'd met him I'd set my heart on working with him during this vacation. There was just something special about him.

"Think he'd be a good young horse project?" Rob asked thoughtfully.

"Ooh," I said, feeling a spark of excitement. "Sure. Maybe. I mean, he's not as far along as our last projects were, though. He's basically a blank slate."

"He's smart and quiet, I think it would be okay. But we'll have to ask a bit more about him."

I tried not to get my hopes up too high, but I was humming under my breath as I led the gelding to the wash rack outside and pulled his saddle off.

He wasn't thrilled to get a bath, he danced around and put his nose in the air to avoid the cool water, but I spoke to him quietly and took my time, and he gradually settled and even seemed to enjoy himself as I massaged shampoo into him.

Once he was squeaky clean, I led him back to his stall and watched him go directly outside for a good roll.

"He's just like you, Red," I said, pausing to scratch Red behind the ears as I headed back outside to help Rob with his next horse. Red was notoriously attracted to anything muddy or messy. Nothing made him happier than covering himself in dirt after a bath.

"Don't worry, you'll always be my favourite boy," I told him as he sniffed my hands and arms carefully all over. I gave his forehead a quick kiss and then went outside to find Rob who was just finishing free lunging the buckskin gelding.

"How has he been?" I asked.

"He's kind enough and obedient, but he's pretty stiff. It's hard to tell but he looks a bit off in the hind end."

I held the horse's reins while Rob swung into the saddle. The gelding looked perfectly fine at the walk and he almost looked okay when he started to trot but after a few laps of our makeshift ring his head began to bob and you could see that one of his hind legs wasn't tracking up nearly as far as the other.

"He's really off," I said but Rob had already pulled the horse up and was patting his neck and swinging to the ground before the words were even out of my mouth.

"That's too bad," he said, "He's a good horse."

"Maybe it's something temporary, like a sprain or a stone bruise."

"Possibly, he felt okay in the walk. I guess we'll have to put him back with the herd now, though. We can't work with him if he's sore."

"So that means we're down two archery horses. Nori's bay mare is the last of our group. If she doesn't pan out then we'll have to pick another one."

"Well, since she wanted to work with that mare herself should we just finish up here and go for a trail ride by ourselves?"

"Yes," I said excitedly. "I can show you the path that runs along the river."

"Should we put the buckskin and the white horse back with the herd first?"

"Not the white one," I said quickly. "Not yet. Just in case he does end up being our project horse, he should stick around a little longer."

Rob laughed and led the buckskin to the wash rack since it wouldn't be very nice to send him back to the herd with his hair still plastered to his neck with margarine residue. The horse was perfectly behaved for his bath and with both of us working on him it didn't take long at all to get him looking fantastic again.

We led him back together and put him out with the herd. His shiny coat and flowing mane and tail were a sharp contrast to the other horses who were still dirty and burr-ridden.

"We really need to do something about these guys," Rob said, "it's not kind to leave them like that. It's got to be uncomfortable."

"Well, we could just do one or two a day until they're all done," I said, "we'd probably have time for that. But not right now, I'm dying for a trail ride."

The whole time I was brushing and tacking Red up in his stall the sheep just quietly ate their hay in the corner, not paying attention to us at all. But the second I opened his door to sneak him out they both made their move. Before I could react, they'd barged out the aisle and onto the grassy area out in front of the barn.

"Hey," I yelled but they ignored me like usual, leaving me to stare after them in frustration. I knew how maddening they could be when they made a break for freedom like that. I doubted that they'd even come back for grain until they got tired of exploring.

"They probably won't go very far," Rob said, laughing. "If you leave the stall door open they might just go back inside on their own."

"Possibly," I said, sighing, but I knew we'd be lucky if they let us catch them again before dark.

Still, there was no help for it unless I wanted to spend a few hours running around in the blazing sun trying to round them up.

"Stay right here," I told them sternly. "And don't cause any trouble."

Portia looked up at me innocently and *baaed,* her voice muffled by the big wad of grass in her mouth. Antonio didn't even bother to respond.

"Right, well, we're off then." I said, leading Red over to the stump we used as a mounting block.

Rob brought Artimax up beside me and we moved off at a leisurely pace, the horses still a little tired after their ride the night before.

Most of the trails that led through the ranch were in open, rolling country with very few trees, but the paths that wound next to the river were in the forest and everything was much cooler in there. The river burbled along beside us and we stopped a few times to watch the miniature waterfalls where rocks and deadfall trees had blocked the current until it had no choice but to spring up overtop of them with a surge of frothy, white water.

"There's the swimming hole Casey told me about." I pointed to the wide, dark pool where someone had dug the river out sideways and made a perfect place to swim that was safe from the rushing current. A massive half-dead tree hung out over the pool and you could see the smooth spot at the end of the trunk where hundreds of feet had worn it smooth over the years using it as a diving platform.

"We should come here to swim this afternoon," Rob said, and I started to say that I didn't even own a bathing suit anymore and that the last time I'd been in the water had been years ago on that disastrous moment at the party when I'd nearly drowned and shamed myself in front of about three hundred people.

A blush stole up my cheeks when I remembered what I'd been like back then, so painfully shy and terrified of what everyone thought of me. That had been before the horses, before Rob, and before I'd broken free from my parents.

"Yes," I answered finally, "that's a good idea." I would swim in shorts and a tank top if I had to. And later when we went to town I would find a bathing suit. I wasn't missing out on anything on this trip.

The trail was winding and full of roots that the horses had to pick their way through carefully so we stuck to a walk and took our time just breathing in the scents and solitude of the forest.

"This is how I want to spend my whole life," I said dreamily, staring up at the leaves overhead.

"Yeah? Not going to the Olympics for archery?" Rob teased. "Not being a dressage queen? Not a horse trainer?"

"Oh, well, those things too, I guess. But then when those things are done, at the end of the day, I just want to be doing this. With you and Red and Artimax. I could never get tired of this."

Rob laughed low under his breath and tilted his head back to look at the patches of blue sky flickering between the trees. "Yeah, me neither," he said finally.

The trail ride put me in a languid, relaxed state of mind so I was not prepared to come back to the barn to see the bay mare, fully tacked up but with her saddle slid sideways and Nori lying on the ground beside her, one foot hanging from the off-side stirrup.

"Oh, no, Nori!"

We were both off our horses and climbing into the ring before I could even blink.

"Help, please," Nori said in a tearful voice. "I'm stuck."

"Easy, mare," Rob said to the bay horse. The mare looked worried but she didn't move when we came over. I held her reins and Rob quickly undid the cinch so the saddle flopped the rest of the way to the ground with a thud.

Nori scrambled backward, using both hands to free her boot where it had been lodged in the stirrup and instantly burst into tears.

"You're okay," I said, kneeling down and wrapping an arm around her shoulders. Her body shuddered a few more times and then she took a deep breath. "What happened?"

"It wasn't her fault," she sniffed. "She was perfect. I just didn't do up that stupid western girth thing tight enough and the saddle slipped. She didn't know what was happening so she scooted forward when I fell and dragged me a bit. But when I screamed, she stopped right away and she hasn't moved this whole time. But I couldn't get loose and I thought you guys were never coming back. I was so scared."

"Does your ankle still hurt?" Rob asked.

"Kind of." Nori sniffled. "But I don't think it's broken or anything. Please don't tell anyone what happened."

Now that I knew she was okay, the reality of what could have happened to her hit me and my fear and relief turned to anger.

"Nori, do you have any idea how dangerous it was for you to work with a strange horse by yourself without anyone around? You could have broken your leg, or worse, you could have broken your neck. You don't know anything about that mare. You are lucky to be in one piece."

Nori's tearstained face reddened and she set her jaw in a determined line. "I know how to ride a horse, Astrid. I'm not stupid."

"Well, apparently you're not that bright either if you didn't make sure your cinch was tight enough and you sneak around riding other people's horses…"

"I wasn't *sneaking*," Nori said furiously. "She's *my* project to work with. You and Rob worked with your horses all morning without anyone supervising. And it's not like you're some hotshot rider. You can't even stomach jumping two feet. Do you know the kind of courses I've ridden?"

"I don't need to be a brilliant rider to know not to ride an unfamiliar horse without anyone else around. That's why Rob and I worked together—"

"Oh, yeah, rub it in. You two are just this perfect couple who do everything together and I'm just alone with nobody because I'm dumb and worthless just like that jerk Jackson said."

Her lower lip trembled and her eyes were full of angry tears. She spun around and tried to storm away but her ankle gave out and she ended up on the ground, crying in pain and frustration.

"Oh, Nori," I said sadly.

"Go away, just leave me here," she sobbed, putting her hands over her face.

"We're not going to leave you," Rob said gently, putting a hand on her shoulder. "Astrid and I are both right here. We're your friends, Nori, and we're part of your barn family, and family looks out for each other."

"And whatever that idiot Jackson said to you was so not true, Nori," I said. "I'm sorry if I sounded mad. I was just so scared when I saw you hanging upside down. The mare is your project but you still can't work with her alone. That goes for all of us. We need to work together as a team with all the horses."

"She was going perfectly until that happened," Nori sniffed. "It wasn't her fault."

"No, that's why it's called an accident," Rob said. "But from now on nobody rides these horses without someone on the ground."

"Fine, "Nori said, sighing heavily.

"It's just like jumping at home," Rob added. "Even Darla wouldn't have wanted you jumping without someone around just in case there was an accident. And she was the world's worst coach when it came to safety."

Darla had been both Rob and Nori's coach when they were both hard into eventing, but from the stories I'd heard she sounded a little unbalanced.

"Oh, she totally was." Nori brightened into laughter. "I remember this one time Lumi didn't want to go into this tiny ditch and she ended up running after him with the lunge whip, yelling like a crazy person. I thought he was going to kick her in the face. It took me forever to get him comfortable with ditches after that."

Her face fell and she sniffled again. "I don't know why she did that. He was such a good horse and he was just a baby."

"Darla had some pretty bad mood swings," Rob said, "that's why I had to stop riding with her. Come on, let's get you up to the house."

"Hang on," I said, "I'm going to bring the truck over here. Then you don't have to walk so far."

It took me a minute to rev the ancient truck to life and roll it as close as I could to the paddock. By the time I was back, Nori had limped her way over to the fence and was standing on the outside clinging to the rails.

I might have agreed not to call Nori's mom and tell on her, but there was no hiding her injury from Aunt Lillian and we couldn't exactly lie about what had happened.

"Well, you can give it a day to see if it gets better, but if it's not improved by tomorrow then we'll need to get it X-rayed," my aunt said when Nori adamantly insisted she didn't need to see a doctor.

Nori was lucky, though. By the time she'd slept the whole afternoon, it was a little less swollen and she could put a tiny bit of weight on it, and by the next day she was only sore. And angry because she still couldn't get her boot on over the swelling.

"Just relax for the day," I told her over breakfast, "read a book, go for a swim."

"But I hate relaxing," Nori said, "that feels wrong when the rest of you are working. I want to be useful."

"Well, there are a whole herd of horses in that paddock who need their manes and tails deburred," Justin said, grinning at her.

"Oh no, anything but that."

"You said you wanted to be useful." He shrugged and sent her a meaningful look.

Nori sighed, groaned and rolled her eyes, but in the end, she spent the whole day working on them.

Justin even brought a chair out for her so she didn't have to stand on her feet all day. She went through four tubs of margarine but the finished result was a herd of gleaming trail horses and not a burr in sight.

While she worked on the ranch horse beautification project, Rob and I took the black mare, the bay mare, and my little white gelding over to the training barn that morning to get them fitted with their own tack, have Justin watch us ride them, and actually find out what their names were.

"Um," Justin said, "the bay is Rocket and the black is Piper, but I actually have no idea who the cremello is. Do you, Liza?"

She shook her head. "I don't recognize him at all. Casey would know, or your dad."

"What did you call him?" I asked Justin. "Crem what?"

"Oh, he's a cremello. It's a cream dilution of chestnut."

"Does that mean there's something wrong with him?"

"No, not at all. It's not that common of a colour though, so I should be able to remember him. We handle them all as babies and he's friendly enough. He looks maybe three or four. Or..." he paused, frowning and then stepped up to run a hand gently over the gelding's shoulder. "Here, fellow, let's check your teeth."

He lifted the horse's upper lip to look at the front of his teeth and then pried his mouth open in one swift move and peered inside. "Yeah, I remember now. He arrived the summer of your Uncle Trent's accident, Astrid. This guy isn't actually one of ours; Trent traded him for one of our colts with a man from the states. He's well-bred and we have his papers. Let me go see what I can find."

He disappeared into the cluttered office and I could hear him rummaging around inside. He finally came back with a big scrap book filled with papers, letters and photos.

"Here's one of the record books for bought horses, ones we didn't breed here ourselves. Here we go. Yep, he's four years old. His registered name is BetYouHitAnIceberg."

"Iceberg?" I said laughing. "He was probably Ice for short."

"Well, you can call him whatever you like," Justin grinned. "It looks like my dad did put a couple beginner rides on him a couple years ago but that he got hurt out in the pasture so had to be turned out for a while. We were pretty overwhelmed after Trent died so I guess he sort of got overlooked. I have no idea how he got in with the ranch horse group, though."

"What sort of injury?" Rob asked.

"It doesn't say. But it couldn't have been too bad. There's no mention of a vet visit and my dad is usually pretty good about recording stuff like that."

"He seemed sound when we free-lunged him," I said hopefully.

"Well, I have a few minutes if you want to bring him into the ring right now and I can take a look at him. But he's too green for the archery clinic. What are you planning to do with him?"

"Well, we thought he might make a good project horse," I said, glancing over at Rob. "Lillian said we could take one or two home with us."

"Fair enough, he's a little greener than he should be at that age, though."

"That's all right. He has a good temperament. I really like him."

"Uh oh, don't go getting too attached. Red will be jealous."

"Yeah, yeah, I know he'd be a sales horse," I said, sighing. "But at least I'd get to work with him in the meantime, right?"

"Yep, that's kind of the attitude we have to have in this business. We can't keep them all."

I looked over at Rob and he shrugged. We were both still feeling the losses of Ellie and Possum.

"Okay, Ice," I said, trying out his name to see if it fit him. "Let's see what you can do."

He wasn't at all nervous in the big ring. He let me lead him around, practicing walk, halt, and backing on the lead a few times and asking him to move his quarters over. Then I slipped off his halter and asked him to move out.

He had a natural brisk movement, tracking up well with his hind end and striding forward easily when I asked him to trot and canter. He had no problem moving in both directions and I didn't see anything that looked like even a hint of lameness.

"Does he look okay?" I asked Justin, just in case I'd missed something.

"Yep, he looks just fine. Want me to pop on and ride him?"

I hesitated just a second too long and I heard him laugh.

"Okay, okay, I get it. He's your project. Put him away then and let's put the other two through their paces."

I felt a little guilty wanting the gelding all for myself, but when I tilted my shoulder inward and Ice turned in immediately off the rail and trotted right up to me, I felt a surge of joy. Only with Red and Quarry had that connection to a horse ever been so strong. I was going to keep that all for myself as long as I was able.

I put Ice in an empty stall while we worked with the bay mare, Rocket, who was exactly as calm and kind as Nori had said. But she was an energetic, forward mover too, and I thought she might be a nice choice for one of the more experienced riders.

The other mare, Piper, was as slow as molasses, though. She trotted and cantered in a leisurely sort of way as if she were a dignified lady who could not be rushed.

"Well, that's five of them sorted," Justin said as he fitted Rocket and Piper with a set of tack of their own. Do you want to pick out another back-up horse just in case?"

"I'm not sure. What do you think?" I turned to Rob.

"I think we're going to have our hands full as it is," he said, raising an eyebrow, "but it's up to you."

"All right, let's risk it. They all seem sound and sane. I think the five we have will be fine."

We rode the mares back to the barn in their newly fitted tack with me leading Ice from Piper's back, an arrangement that neither of them seemed to mind. We weren't quite ready to stop riding so we let the horses saunter over to the corral where Nori was just finishing up cleaning up the ranch horses we hadn't used.

"Wow, they look great," Rob said.

"Yeah, well, they should. That took me forever. Thank goodness for that margarine trick. It would have taken me years to finish without that. Mara and Casey said they'd help me give them proper baths tonight after work."

"That was nice of them," I said, reaching down to take the lead rope out of Ice's teeth. It was soggy where he'd chewed it.

"So, what's going to happen to these ranch horses now if there's nobody around to use them?" Nori asked, glancing over at the herd behind her. "You think there is any chance of them selling to good homes before the auction? I'd hate for them to end up there. They're such nice horses."

"I'm not sure," I told her honestly. "Maybe we could take some pictures of them once they're all cleaned up and put them on the Triple Hills website. There's a chance we could sell them on there first."

"They're well-trained and even tempered," Rob said reassuringly. "That type of horse is probably in demand."

"Huh." Nori leaned her elbows on the fence and reached through the bars to tickle the bay mare's nose. "Then why are they still here if they're easy to sell?"

"I think Aunt Lillian just sort of forgot them," I said. "But I mean, they're fed, they have an amazing pasture, and they get their feet done regularly. That's more than a lot of horses have. It's not like they're completely abandoned.

"They still shouldn't just be forgotten," Nori said stubbornly, "they're good horses."

There wasn't much more we could say about that and our concerns were temporarily forgotten anyway when we dragged ourselves inside for an early dinner.

It was just us and Aunt Lillian that night, and the second we sat down at the table to devour our giant bowls of spaghetti, Aunt Lillian set a stapled stack of papers about an inch thick next to each of us.

"There's the list of everything you need to know about the circus of chaos that is about to descend on us."

Circus of chaos? I thought, laughing under my breath. *That's a little dramatic.* But as I flipped through the sheets I suddenly realized what a big undertaking this was to organize. No wonder she'd asked for our help.

"I've written down the basic details on the five riders who will be using our horses. Keep them in mind while you work with the animals so you can try to make a good match between each horse and rider. The remaining riders will bring their own horses, of course. There is a list of them here too, so you'll want to make sure there are stalls available for them and room in the tack room for all their things.

"I'll be busy trying to figure out where they're all going to sleep and how we're supposed to feed everyone. Thank goodness some of them want to camp."

She paused to eat for a few minutes, still frowning down at the sheet in front of her.

"The clinic itinerary is there, too. There will be two groups, beginner and advanced, and each group will have two lessons a day. At the beginning, half the lessons will be about archery skills on the ground without the horses. As the clinic progresses, the horses will be used for both morning and afternoon lessons, but there won't be much speed work so they shouldn't feel overworked at all."

"Then of course there will be a small, friendly competition at the end during the ah, the festival. The Society people will be doing a jousting match and other non-horse things as well that will all tie in together over the festival weekend. There should be a fair amount of spectators, too."

"Okay," I said, leafing through the sheets with one hand. "I think we can handle this, right?"

I looked at Rob and Nori, who nodded reassuringly.

"The horses are doing well and we can set up a real archery course tomorrow to start walking them through it."

"That's another thing," Aunt Lillian said, "we can't stop our regular lessons and training in the indoor for a whole week to accommodate this clinic, and Laszlo said that he preferred a more realistic outdoor setting anyway. So we'll have to find a flat area outside where we can section off a ring-sized area. Something with decent footing that's not too far from the barn. Maybe you guys can start scouting around."

"The pasture out behind the broodmare barn could work," Rob said, "we've been letting the horses out there to graze and they've beaten it down a little."

"Right, well, let me know what you decide. If there are grass and weeds that need to be cut down then we have a mower deck that hooks up to the tractor that you can use. And don't forget that there are some targets to be built and that weird moving horse thing."

"Weird horse thing?" I asked.

"Yes, um, I believe it's on page 27." She flipped through the pages until she found the one she wanted. "See, right there, barrel horse on wheels. I don't get it."

"Horse on wheels." I flipped through the pages in front of me until I found the rough set of drawings that Lazlo Belko had sent to Aunt Lillian. He wasn't the best artist and it took me a minute to sort it out.

"Oh, that must be the thing Justin was talking about. It looks like a kind of trailer that's meant to be pulled behind a truck or something. See, he's got a barrel fixed to it and then you attach a fake horse neck and head to it. You can practice shooting off it first to get used to the feeling of something moving underneath you and don't risk hurting the horses. It's kind of brilliant, actually. It would be perfect for beginners."

"Well, I think it's a bit much for him to ask us to construct something so complicated. I mean, we do have an old trailer, but I'd have no idea how to put it together."

"I'm not sure it will be that hard. If we can find the barrel then Rob and I could build the horse head and neck. That can't be too difficult. And we could mount an old saddle on it. Rob has a woodworking shop at home so he's used to working with all the tools. And I'm good at painting. I think we could make something half-decent."

"Well, if you think you have the time, then I'll leave you to it. I can't say how thankful I am to have you here, Astrid. You kids are doing some great work. I'm impressed and I wish you could stay with me year-round."

The next morning was much more relaxed than our previous days had been. At least the pressure of having to choose and clean up our horses was done and now we could get down to the business of slowly conditioning them and making sure they were a hundred percent comfortable around the archery equipment.

All three of us worked each horse together this time. Nori still wasn't up to riding, but she helped us groom and watched each of the sessions carefully. And she was the one who set up the target outside the paddock and practiced shooting while we double-checked the horses' reactions to the hiss and *thunk* of the arrows.

None of the ranch horses were remotely alarmed by anything we did and by the end of the session, each of them could be trusted to walk in a straight line outside the paddock, past the target, while Rob and I shot off their backs. We would wait for higher speeds once we had our outdoor course set up.

When it came time to work with Ice, I first free-lunged him at a walk and trot in the little paddock, letting him get used to Red's lighter dressage saddle. I'd left the stirrups dangling to see how he reacted to the light banging on his side but he didn't seem to mind.

"Wow, you look so handsome, Ice," I told him. "You'll make a fancy little dressage horse someday."

"I know he's four but I think he's still got a bit of growing to do," Rob said thoughtfully. "I think he's going to be a nice horse."

"Well, you're already a nice horse, aren't you?" I crooned to

Ice as I brought him into the middle of the ring. "Today we're just going to work on walking and steering, though. We'll save the trot for later."

I fitted Red's bridle over his head, glad they were roughly the same size. I only had to adjust a few buckles to make it fit properly.

He stood perfectly still as I got on and I gave him a minute to adjust to the feeling of a new saddle. Western saddles did a good job of distributing the rider's weight over a big area, all across the horse's back, where a dressage saddle had much narrower points of contact where the weight sat. The horse was supposed to be able to feel the rider's seat aids very clearly.

Because of this, I had to remember to sit very light in the saddle and not put too much pressure on Ice's undeveloped back.

We moved off at the walk and I was pleased to see that he was completely unfazed by the new tack. I just had him walk around the edge of the paddock and not worry too much about steering at first. When I felt his back relax and his head drop, I gently opened my inside rein, shifted my weight slightly, and asked for a change of direction. I would have to keep things very basic with him for a while.

He was a lot more comfortable than he had been for our first ride together so I was able to switch directions a few times and do some figure eights. When he'd done all that, I brought him gently to a halt and gave him an enthusiastic pat.

"That looked really good, Astrid," Rob said. "Much better than last time."

"Yeah," I said, sliding to the ground and giving Ice another good scratch on the neck. "It helps that we know he's a baby horse. I don't think he had any idea what I was asking him to do last time. He was just doing his best to guess."

After I hopped off, we led him outside the paddock and Nori fired off a few arrows. When he didn't react, I shot a few with him standing beside me. I took my time, making sure he was standing in a safe spot and that he didn't move or fidget when I took aim.

For the most part he behaved very well, although he did try to keep nibbling my bow, my arrows, the quiver. Pretty much anything he could get his lips on.

The three of us had already decided that we needed a break from working in the heat of the day again. Rob and I had made plans to ride with Liza that night. I was finally getting her to give me my first lesson on Red and she'd asked Rob to ride one of her horses for her.

Nori and Maverick were heading out on another trail ride with Casey and Mara after dinner.

So we took the afternoon off and lazed away drinking iced tea on the front porch where it was covered from the sun and a gentle breeze filtered in through the trees. Nori had found some cowboy romance book I was sure her mom would not approve of and had curled up in a chair with her bare feet up on the railing and her eyes fixed intently on the page.

Rob and I gathered up snacks and drinks, pads of papers and pens, and commandeered the big porch swing together where we both sat cross-legged facing each other with the paper spread out between us.

We had Aunt Lillian's list of all the riders who were bringing their own horses plus a list of those participants who were riding our horses. It was easy for some of them to see who would be in the beginning section and who would be in the advanced, but some of them were not so clear. It was hard to mesh two completely different skills into one clinic. Someone could be a top level archer and yet had never sat on a horse. Which category would they fall into? It's pretty hard to be a safe, accurate shooter when you can't control your horse or you keep falling off.

We could pencil in which riders and horses might be a good match, but we couldn't know for sure until they actually got here and we could get an idea of their personalities and skill levels.

We didn't even really know the horses that well yet. I was sure we'd find personality quirks as the weeks progressed.

"Well, at least we've made a beginning," Rob said. "We have the horses, we have the riders. Now we just need to get all the equipment ready. It's like a puzzle."

"You're having fun with this, aren't you?" I asked, grinning.

"Yes," he said, smiling. "Aren't you?"

"I am. It's totally different and a little stressful, and I don't want to mess up and let Aunt Lillian down, but other than that it's pretty fun."

Rob laughed and reached out and linked one of my hands with his. "You're such a worrier."

"I am. I truly am. But I really am having fun. I'm glad you're here with me."

"I'm glad you're here with me, too."

"Well, I'm glad that you're glad that I'm..."

"Okay, you two, knock it off," Nori growled from her corner of the deck. "Some of us are trying to read."

We both snickered and I reached out impulsively, put both of my hands on Rob's shoulders and kissed him firmly. Which would have been better if we hadn't been on a swing because I nearly sent both of us toppling off sideways in a fit of laughter.

"Sorry if we're interrupting your smutty romance novel, Nori."

"It's historical," she said defensively. "And it has horses."

"Uh-huh. And I guess that poor guy with the glistening chest on the cover just happened to misplace his shirt somewhere."

"He's a cowboy," Nori said furiously.

"Sure, sure, whatever you say."

It was a good way to spend an afternoon.

As soon as I knew Liza was taking her break I went and grabbed her painting from the tack room where it had sat for days. There just hadn't been a good time to get it to her and I'd wanted to catch her alone. We were supposed to meet up to have some snacks and catch up a little.

Liza and Justin had bought a huge RV trailer that they'd parked behind the training barn. I'd caught sight of it the day before but I hadn't been inside yet and now I paused at the small screen door, wondering whether I should knock or ring the bell.

"Oooh, Astrid, come on in," Liza called as she caught sight of me just standing there indecisively on her porch. She pushed open the screen door and waved me inside.

"I brought your painting," I said, holding it up.

"I'm so excited to see it. I have no idea what it could be. Do you?"

"No." I shook my head and climbed the metal steps until I was inside. "She made one for me too, but she wouldn't show me yet. She didn't tell me what she was working on. Wow, this is amazing in here."

"Pretty luxurious, hey? All leather furniture and a fireplace, too. We weren't sure whether to get one of these or a tiny home but we knew we didn't want to live up in the bunk house anymore. This is a perfect starter home. And it's portable, too."

She laughed and ushered me into the cozy living room where there was a little platter of tea on the table and a plate full of cake slices.

"This looks great, Liza. Thanks."

"It's not homemade but it is delicious. Better eat your fill before Justin comes home. He'll polish off whatever's left in under a minute. That man is always hungry."

"Thank you," I said, handing her the case, "here, you'd better take this. Hopefully it made the trip safely."

Liza set the case on her lap while I helped myself to a cake. She clicked the metal snaps open and slowly lifted the lid. She pulled out the paper-wrapped canvas and then quickly moved the case to the floor. The paper was glued down to itself so she had to tear it and it made a little scritching sound as she carefully peeled the layers away.

"Oh wow," she said, and I moved over to stand beside her so I could get a better look.

It wasn't what I'd expected. I'd sort of assumed it would be a realistic painting of Liza riding Marcus or Folly, or one of the fancy dressage horses she'd ridden in Germany. But instead it was a more abstract painting of a girl in a long, pale blue dress, standing with her arms outstretched in a green field.

The features weren't quite clear but you could see that she was smiling and had her eyes closed, and you had the *feeling* that it was Liza even if it didn't completely look like her.

And galloping around the figure, like a blur of carousel ponies, was a circle of whirling horses, white, grey, and blue, moving so fast that they nearly blended in with the background. It was completely unexpected but also perfect. Like it was meant for Liza and no one else.

"This—" Liza's voice broke for a second and she had to stop and wipe her eyes, "this is incredible. I need to call her. I need to thank her."

"I'll go," I said, rising to my feet. I hated to cut any visit with Liza short, but she obviously wanted to talk to Oona. "I should check on the sheep anyway. I left them grazing on their own."

"Thank you, Astrid. Don't forget that you and Rob are coming up for lessons tonight after dinner."

She'd already turned away to go find her phone and, after swiping a final slice of cake from the plate, I headed back out into the sunshine.

Our plans for lessons after dinner were abruptly derailed when Aunt Lillian announced that tonight was the night we'd have to send Antonio off to live in the hills with the other sheep.

"I saw that animal trying to butt my truck tires today, Astrid. Today is the day he leaves."

Despite the fact that I'd known this was going to happen, and that I knew it was going to be the best thing for him, I still felt my eyes prickle with tears.

Sure, he was bad sometimes, but I'd raised him from a tiny baby. I'd watched him being born. So it was hard to think of sending him away.

"We'll load him in the trailer right after dinner and take him out there. Is he locked up already?"

"Yes, he came in when we fed the horses their grain."

"Good. That will make it easier. Bryce is going to help us. The lamb is still young enough that he'll be able to just pick him up and pop him in the trailer."

"All right," I said with a sigh.

"Don't worry. He might not like the trailer ride, but he'll have fun once he's up in the hills. The band he's going with doesn't have a ram in with it yet so he won't get beaten up."

I didn't say much after that, just ate my food and listened to Nori telling Aunt Lillian all about how good the ranch horses looked now that they'd been cleaned up. I had the feeling that Nori was now on a mission to save her new friends from auction.

"Do you want me to come with you?" Rob asked after dinner. "I can find Liza now and tell her I can't make my lesson."

"Oh, no, I'll be fine," I said. "Go ride. Be brilliant. I'll come over afterward if it's not too late."

"Mara and I are going for a quick trail ride," Nori said. "She's lending me her western saddle to try."

"Oh, are you switching over to the dark side?" Rob laughed.

"Ha ha," she said sarcastically. "No, but they're definitely more comfortable to trail ride in. And I might try using it for some archery too."

My palms were sweating as we drove down to the broodmare barn in Aunt Lillian's truck, the small wooden livestock trailer rattling along behind us. Even though this was the best thing for everyone I still felt guilty. And I wondered if Portia was going to be sad and miss him. What if she pined away for him and stopped eating?

"Throw some grain in a bucket so they're distracted," my aunt said in a businesslike voice. "Bryce will just pick him up and put him in the trailer. You'd better take his collar off too, he can't wear it out when he's loose on the range, it could get caught on something and choke him.

The second there was food in front of them Antonio didn't even notice when I unbuckled his collar. He didn't really care that much when Bryce scooped him up and put him in the trailer either. I'd already put a bucket of grain and some hay in the trailer so he just started eating without even looking around at his new surroundings. He was the definition of "food motivated."

And Portia, instead of being devastated like I'd worried she'd be to see her son leave, just kept hoovering up the grain he'd left behind without even looking up.

"Nice, Portia," I told her, "that's super loyal of you."

She grunted as I scratched her behind the ear and then went up to Red's manger to start in on his hay.

"Come on, Astrid, let's not keep him waiting," my aunt called.

The roads to Antonio's new pasture were overgrown, rutted paths, and I winced as the trailer bumped and lurched its way along, hoping that Antonio would survive the trip.

He'd only *baaed* once at the start of the journey, but after that he'd been silent.

"There they are, Astrid," Bryce said, pointing to the field off to the right.

A flock of fat white sheep was grazing in a little hollow where the grass was growing about two feet tall. A few of them looked up as we approached but most were focused on eating. Nearby a familiar grey shape was also grazing.

"Hey, it's Donkey," I said in surprise, recognizing my old friend.

"Oh, yes, he's on guard duty with this flock. The plan is to get livestock dogs to watch the sheep eventually, but in the meantime this guy will do," Aunt Lillian said approvingly.

One of the sheep let out a low *baa* and Antonio immediately answered from inside the trailer, sounding muffled.

"Well, let's let him out, Astrid. It sounds like he's ready."

Bryce worked the rusty trailer latch free and then motioned for me to open the door. It swung back and Antonio stood there looking around in astonishment, a tuft of hay hanging from his mouth. His eyes widened even more when he caught sight of the other sheep. He stared for another few seconds and then leapt down out of the trailer, trotting over to them without even looking back.

The ewe nearest to him lowered her head as he approached and then gave him a hefty butt in the side when he got too close, nearly knocking him over.

"Hey, stop that," I said, worried that he'd get hurt.

"That's how they sort things out," my aunt said. "He'll figure it out."

He scrambled to his feet and approached her again, this time more cautiously. And, when she lowered her head again to threaten him he just turned away and began to nibble at the grass nearby.

The big sheep glared at him for a second and then started eating as well.

"And that's pretty much all it takes with sheep," Bryce said, "they're very tolerant of newcomers who mind their manners."

We stood out there watching for a little bit longer, until the mosquitos arrived and drove us back to the truck.

Antonio didn't even look up as we left.

Back at the barn, I spent a long time just hanging out and brushing Red and Portia. Neither of them seemed sad or showed any sign of missing their friend so far and I wondered how animals processed things like loss. Did they wonder what had happened to him? Did they think he'd be back? If I ever did decide to go to university after high school then animal behaviour was one thing I could see myself studying. They were so different than us and yet we had so much in common.

Someone like my dad would hardly give an animal credit for having feelings at all. To him, animals were one step up from a stuffed toy. Just there to take for walks, use, or compete with but not as having intricate social lives.

It wasn't until I'd spent so much time around the horses and sheep that I realized how truly complex animals were.

CHAPTER 14

Rob had been right about the pasture behind the broodmare barn. It was large and relatively flat, and the horses and Portia had done a good job already of mowing down the tall grass. Aunt Lillian gave us a demonstration on how to use one of the smaller tractors and we took turns driving it carefully around the field with the temperamental mower deck churning along behind it.

We tried to mow in straight lines but it didn't help that Portia had come with us and kept grazing right in front of it without moving whenever we were finishing a row.

We managed to get it done though and soon, the air was fragrant with the sweet smell of newly cut grass and we were both spattered in little green bits that clung to our arms faces and clothes.

It's a good thing I'm wearing old clothes, I thought, looking down at myself.

Once it was mowed flat, it was easier to envision it as a grassy outdoor ring.

"This will work well," I said. "We can set up the targets in the middle so the archers can shoot inwards. Then there won't be any risk of shooting anyone."

"Do we have enough targets?" Rob asked.

"Er, probably not. I only have the two foam ones I brought. And I'm sure we could steal some from the archery range, too. We should probably see what Mr. Belko wants us to have set up and then we can make some if we need to. As long as we have time to get supplies."

I bit my lip, thinking of all the things we needed to get done. Three weeks had seemed like forever to get organized for one little clinic, but now I could almost feel the minutes ticking away.

"We're in good shape," Rob said, guessing my thoughts. "We just need to keep moving steadily along. We should set up the targets we do have and start working the horses in here so they're used to it, though."

"Good idea."

The targets were easy enough to set up and we found some plastic stakes that were meant for temporary fencing to stick in the ground about twelve feet out from the perimeter fence line. When the clinic date was closer we would string a rope from post to post making a long, narrow channel for the riders to gallop down while they shot at the targets. This made it easier for them to drop the reins to shoot because the horses would—hopefully—just continue in a straight line down the channel right to the end without stopping or swerving.

"Now don't touch those, Portia," I told her, as she began to experimentally use one of the plastic stakes to itch her shoulder on. I had the feeling that we would be spending the next few weeks replacing these poles every time they were knocked down.

Nori was feeling well enough to take over riding the bay mare, Rocket, so we took three of the horses and practiced walking, trotting, and cantering them down the channels. They were the most placid, laid back horses who took everything in stride. We walked them around the field a few times, then trotted and cantered on a loose rein, and then practiced dropping our reins at all three gaits.

"These horses are amazing," Nori said. "Why are they so good? Especially when they had a whole season off of work?"

"A combination of breeding and initial training, I think," Rob said. "Most of the horses that I've met here are like this."

"Well, it's a little weird."

"You're lucky they're so good, otherwise, your little accident the other day could have been much worse," Rob reminded her.

"Right. Good point."

After we'd warmed them up, we started with the archery. First taking turns leading the horses on foot and shooting our two targets. Then again at the walk with someone leading the horse while the archer shot. The horses had been used to us shooting around them for the last few days so we didn't expect anyone to be too nervous, but it was always best to take our time and make sure they were really one hundred percent confident.

We graduated to walking them through on their own, then trotting in, dropping to a walk, shooting and then back up to a trot again. Then we trotted all the way through and finally did it at a canter. The horses all took it completely in stride and seemed to enjoy their morning out.

Then we had to put them away and do it all over again with the next group of horses. Nori rode the paint and Rob had the black mare, and that left me with my project Ice.

He wasn't up to all the speed work yet, and quite honestly, I wasn't ready to canter a horse that was so green, but I let him walk and trot around the field with the others and he was perfectly well-behaved, although unbalanced at the trot and a little unsure about downward transitions.

I took him into the center of the field while the others cantered and he didn't fuss at all while his friends ran. He just stood there, watching them with interest and enjoying the neck scratches I was giving him.

"You're more like a unicorn than a horse," I told him. "You're just like Red, kind of perfect."

He snorted and bobbed his nose a little, probably in response to a fly or something but it felt like he was agreeing with me.

Once the others were warmed up we did the same thing with this group as we did with the last, first shooting on foot and then graduating to under saddle.

Ice was great for the on-foot part, except he kept turning his nose around to nibble at my bow and my arrows. I had to keep patiently moving him out of my space. As cute and innocent as he was being, it could also be dangerous if he bumped me with his nose just as I was shooting.

For the under saddle part, I had Rob lead him at a walk and wait until he was still before I took each shot; he was way too interested in turning around to nibble on my boots or go after inviting looking clumps of grass than stand still and be patient. But he certainly wasn't scared of anything that I was doing on his back.

We got back to the barn glowing with happiness on how our group was progressing. If they kept on like this we'd have some serious mounted archery horses by the time our month here was up.

CHAPTER 15

Aunt Lillian was on the front porch waiting for us when I finally rolled the truck into the driveway.

"Astrid, come quickly," she said, practically jumping up and down with excitement.

I groaned inwardly, thinking that it was just more clinic stuff she'd forgotten to tell us. She was always springing new chores on me last minute. We'd had a whole day of working and riding, and I was exhausted. All I wanted was a hot shower, some food, and my bed.

"Hurry," she said, "Marion's on the phone for you. It's about the baby."

My heart stopped hard in my chest and there was a second there where I thought I'd throw up. Rob met my panicked gaze and it was his warm smile and encouraging nod that gave me enough courage to hurry up the porch steps and follow Aunt Lillian into the house.

It has to be bad news. She wouldn't call if it wasn't. I know it.

"Here she is," Lillian was saying loudly into the old wall phone. "She's right here, Marion."

"Astrid." Her voice sounded very tired but it was as warm and kind as always, and it was all I needed to burst into tears. "It's all right. They released the baby today from ICU. We brought her home. We've named her Aurora."

I was having trouble saying anything at all so it was lucky that Marion kept on talking.

"She's a real fighter, just like you. And your father and I so thankful we could bring her home with us. We can't wait for you to meet her. We both love you so much."

I was so overwhelmed by emotion that my mind went a complete blank.

"I like the name Aurora," I managed to say, my voice sounding strange and ragged in my ears.

"It has a special meaning to us, too," Marion said dreamily, "she was conceived on a magical winter night of passion under the northern lights. Breathtaking."

Luckily she didn't seem to notice the gagging, choking noise I made at the words *conceive* and *passion*. Not something anyone needed to picture their parents involved with. Ever. And now my poor half-sister was going to be saddled with that story for the rest of her life. My tears dried up instantly.

"Congratulations," I told her. "Really. I'm so glad she's doing better."

"She'll need a little extra support for a few weeks but the doctors think she'll do just fine. Your father and I are planning a road trip south next month, just as soon as the doctor says it's okay. We told Lillian that we're going to stop in and visit you in person for a couple of days. That would be all right, wouldn't it?"

"Um, okay. That would be, uh, nice. I guess," I said hesitantly, because, as happy as I was that Aurora was going to be okay, I still didn't want to see my parents. There was a reason I'd cut them out of my life permanently.

Marion sighed heavily down the line and I immediately felt guilty. surely one weekend visit wouldn't be the end of the world.

I'd meet the baby and then they'd go safely back to Alaska where they belonged.

"Well, it would be nice to see you, Astrid. It's been a while. And I know you'll want to meet your sister."

"Uh, yeah. Are you sure it's safe for her to travel, though?"

"We'll only plan to come if she's well enough. We have a few weeks to decide. I'd better go though, darling. She's waking up. Give my love to Lillian and everyone."

I heard a tiny mewling cry like a kitten might make and then the line disconnected abruptly.

"Well," I said, hanging up the bulky plastic receiver. "That was interesting."

"The baby's okay, then? Everyone is fine?"

"Ah, yes. They said they want to come and visit before I go back to the Island."

"Are you sure you're okay with that?" my aunt asked me anxiously. "Marion actually asked me first before you came in, but I didn't agree to anything. I wanted it to be your decision."

"I think it's okay," I said, but now I wasn't sure why I'd said yes. I didn't want them or the baby in my life, no matter how briefly and I wasn't sure why I hadn't told Marion that on the phone.

I walked out of the kitchen still in a daze, my mind whirling in a million different directions, all thoughts of a shower and bed pushed aside. I went out to the porch instead and when I found Rob waiting for me there, the relief I felt was overwhelming. His face was shadowed in the dying light, but he opened his arms and I walked into them like a storm-ravaged boat reaching a safe harbour and promptly burst into tears again.

"You're okay," was all he said as he pulled me down onto the porch swing with his arms still wrapped tightly around me and he let my cry out all my old fears. Because the thought of seeing them again was like reliving that terrifying night I'd run away all over again. My heart was beating a million miles an hour and it was a long time before I calmed down enough to feel how warm and strong his arms were around me, and how steady his heart beat was, and that I was here, in this good, safe place with people who loved me and not alone at all. Gradually, the terror seeped away and I drew in a deep shuddering sigh.

We shifted sideways so that we were leaning back against the swing with Rob's shoulder cushioning my head, one arm still wrapped around me and the other pushing my hair back from my face in a steady soothing motion. I tilted my head back to look at the dark sky, watching as the stars came out one by one. First there was just a couple and then suddenly the whole sky was blanketed in them.

"Her name is Aurora," I said quietly.

"That's a nice name."

"I'm glad she's going to be okay, but I don't want to see them."

"Then don't. You can change your mind."

"I think I'm going to see them even though I don't want to. I should do this. I should meet the baby at least once. She's my sister."

"Yes," he said slowly, "she is. But, the nice thing about being an adult is that you get to *choose* your family, Astrid. They don't have to be in your life just because they're blood."

I nodded, understanding exactly what he was saying. Rob was more my family than my dad or Marion had ever been. So was *his* dad, who'd worried about me and fussed over me way more than my own family ever had. So were Hilary and the Ahlbergs, who'd taken me in when I'd run away, and my barn family and Aunt Lillian and Liza and Justin. All those people were what family was supposed to be. Loving and supportive.

"I love you," I said spontaneously. And even though it came out before I'd thought about it, and Rob's fingers froze on my cheek and he didn't answer for what felt like a lifetime, I was still glad I'd said it. Because I'd realized suddenly that it was the truth.

No matter how he felt about me, I loved him more than I'd ever loved another human and I wasn't taking it back.

"Astrid," he said, his voice sounding distorted.

"It's okay," I said. I was too tired to care about hurt feelings right then.

In answer he ran his fingers down my jaw and tilted my head back until his lips were just millimeters from mine.

"I've loved you from the moment I saw you at that party," he whispered. "The second you stepped onto that rope swing."

Then he kissed me. And it wasn't like our other kisses, all sweet and light and tingly. This was deeper, full of meaning and passion and the secrets of the universe unravelling. It was like stepping out of the desert into the ocean. It was like our souls had known each other for a hundred lifetimes. It could have lasted for seconds or hours, but when we finally came up for air, something had shifted and I felt suddenly like a different person, older and wiser and just...different.

I stared up at the planes of his face, chiseled and otherworldly in the dim porch light, like he was a statue of an ancient god of the woods or something.

"You're beautiful," I told him, because apparently it was my night for spontaneous sharing.

"No, *you're* beautiful," he said laughing, his hand inching down to tickle my ribs.

"No, you," I said, twisting away from him before he could start tickling because that was a game I always lost.

"We need to get some food."

"Aunt Lillian is probably wondering what happened to me."

"Come on," he swung himself upright suddenly and pulled me to my feet. For a second I was against his chest again, feeling his familiar heartbeat and the warmth that radiated off of him, and then my stomach growled in hunger and we were laughing again, the mood half-broken but still lingering and we went inside to find some food.

CHAPTER 16

"Aunt Lillian, I we need to run to town for a few supplies," I told her over breakfast that morning. "We were thinking of working on the targets and that barrel horse thing today."

Aunt Lillian had recently gotten a long-winded email from Laszlo Belko, and he'd said that the few foam targets we'd scrounged up were not enough. We'd need five big targets on posts at different heights. But, thankfully, had also given us some direction for making them. It was just one more thing to add to the list of chores we had to do.

"Oh, sure, sure. Justin said he was going to do a feed run today so maybe you can all go along with him."

"Thanks, I was thinking maybe we could go for lunch to that diner, too. I wanted to show it to Rob and Nori."

"Well, that sounds like a good idea. Maybe you could take Mara along with you, too."

"Okay, I'll go ask her after breakfast."

While Rob and Nori started in on the first horses of the morning, I went down to the training barn to track down Mara.

I found her in a stall carefully tacking up a cute little grey mare.

"Hey, Mara."

"Hey." She looked up guardedly, still not trusting me after all this time.

"We're going to town for lunch and we wondered if you'd like to come. We're just doing some shopping at the hardware store and going to the diner."

"Oh," she said, tightening the cinch slowly. "I guess I could ask Liza if I could get away for a little bit. If you really want me to come along."

"Yes, of course we do. It will be fun."

"Right, okay, thanks."

She smiled at me tentatively and I drove back up to the smaller barn wondering what on earth had happened to change Mara so much since I'd last been here. Yeah, she'd been a thug before but she'd also been bold and confident and full of life. Now she just seemed … sad.

We worked with our horses all morning and then hurried up to the house to clean up.

"We have our list of supplies?" I asked Rob.

"Yep, right here. I want to pop into the gift store and get some sort of souvenir for my dad, too.

When Justin's truck pulled up, I was happy to see that Liza was with him, too. It was nice that everyone could take a break to get away now and then.

Triple Hills the town was set in a deep valley next to a lake and when we reached the top of the steep hill that led into town, I was practically bouncing up and down in excitement. After being on the ranch non-stop it was a treat to see civilization again.

As soon as we came down the hill, all of our phones began to ping in unison as a slew of backed up messages, texts, and emails came pouring in.

We all jumped, fishing out our phones as if it was an emergency even though if anyone really needed to reach us they could just use the land line.

Most of the people who I wanted to talk to were in the truck with me right then so, after a brief glance I shoved my phone away again. I would check it properly once we were at the restaurant.

The town was pretty much exactly the same as when I'd seen it last, the quaint little shops frozen in time. There were no big box stores here. For that you'd have to drive to the next town over.

We pulled in front of the hardware store first.

"Are you coming, Nori?" I asked as the rest of us piled out. Justin and Liza were going to run to the feed store while the rest of us were shopping.

She was still sitting stone-still on her seat, hunched over her phone with a look of growing panic on her face.

"Nori, are you okay?"

"What? Um, yeah, I'm coming." She shoved her phone in her pocket and slid out of the truck, slamming the door hard behind her.

She smiled briefly as she brushed quickly past me, but her eyes were wide and her face was pale. She looked like she'd had a shock.

Rob glanced at me questioningly, but I just shrugged. I had no idea what was going on, either.

We were the only customers in the hardware store and our boots clomped loudly on the wooden floors as we marched up and down the aisles, working our way through the list.

We had lots of scrap wood back at the ranch and we'd managed to find a wooden barrel, but we needed paint and some things to construct the new targets.

"Are you finding everything you need?" A little bent, white-haired man hobbled over to us, supporting himself on a metal cane.

"I think so," I said, "we just need to get the paint now."

"Well, that's at the front here. You're from up at the ranch, aren't you? You're that archery girl who belongs to Lillian."

"Uh, that's right." I laughed. "I'm her niece."

"I remember you from when you came in here last time you visit. You helped my grandson, Lincoln, with that archery stuff he's always going on about."

"Oh, are you Lincoln's grandpa? I haven't seen him yet since I've been back. I saw that he's doing the horse archery clinic coming up, though."

"Oh, yes. His new girlfriend talked him into it. She's a shy little thing, but she's determined once she gets an idea in her head. Lincoln's been visiting his other grandparents in the city but he should be back any day. I'll let him know you said hello."

By the time we'd picked everything out, Justin and Liza were back and we took a minute to pile all our supplies in the back of the truck around the stacks of feed bags.

"Won't someone steal our stuff if it's just sitting out in the back of the truck like that?" Nori asked.

"Not here," Liza said, grinning at Nori's skeptical look. "I know. It took me a while to get used to, too. But everyone knows everyone here and, on a slow day in town, there's not much else to do but look out the windows. Anyone stealing would get caught for sure. The sheriff would probably show up at their house before they'd even made it home.

The diner was packed but we managed to find a booth that fit all of us in the back corner by the window. Just like the town, the diner looked exactly like I remembered and when the smiling waitress brought our menus, I was pretty sure all the food was the same, too. It probably hadn't changed in twenty years.

"Hey everyone," the waitress said, "today's special is our half-price beef-dip sandwiches. Coffee all around?"

She was pouring the black liquid into our mugs before we'd even answered, flapping our menus down one by one in front of each of us with her other hand.

"Good to see you, cousin," she added, giving Mara's shoulder a squeeze. "We've missed you at family dinners. You ever need anything you give us a call, okay?"

"Okay, thanks," Mara mumbled, staring down at her menu.

While we waited for our food we took full advantage of the free Wi-Fi at the diner. There was about fifteen solid minutes of silence while we all dealt with the messages on our phones. Even Liza and Justin were busy tapping away. Technically there was dial-up at the ranch, but it was so painfully slow that it was hardly worth the effort.

I scrolled through Hillary's messages and texts and sent her a billion photos of the horses at the ranch and gave her a brief update on what we were doing. I also sent her a photo of me and Ice that had a heart around it. I was still going to have to figure out how to broach the subject of me bringing another horse home.

Rob and I set our phones down at exactly the same time and looked around blinking at our surroundings, like we were coming up for air.

"Good timing." Rob laughed. "The food is here."

I'd ordered a burger, but in this place that also came with a huge serving of fries, onion rings, and a small salad. Enough carbs to last a lifetime.

We dug into our food and it wasn't until I was partway through my burger that I noticed that Nori was hardly eating. Instead, she was hunched over her phone with a look of pure misery on her face.

"Oh, my gosh, Nori, what's wrong?" I asked.

But instead of answering she just shook her head and wiped a hand furiously across her eyes.

"Nothing. It's nothing."

"It's not nothing," I persisted. "Seriously, what is the matter?"

"Oh, it's just—" she looked around the table for second and then sighed. "Okay, fine. It's just these stupid kids at school. There was this guy and well, I thought he liked me. But I guess he didn't because he got mad at me and now he's…"

She took in a deep shuddering breath and Mara reached out and squeezed her arm gently.

"I thought it would stop after school was done, but he won't leave me alone. He made this stupid page and he put up all these awful paintings and sketches of me. He releases one a week and it's this big thing that everyone finds hilarious. They're all over the internet."

"Nori," Liza said seriously, "that's actually harassment. You could press charges for something like that. It's right up there with stalking. You should really talk to your mom about this."

"No way, she'd kill me if she knew about this. Some of the paintings are just silly to make me look ugly or dumb, but some of them are creepy and they make me look like I hardly have any clothes on. I only posed for him a couple of times and I certainly wasn't naked, but the way he paints is so realistic. Nobody would believe me. That's why he got mad at me in the first place because I wouldn't pose for him like that. He said he'd make me pay unless I did what he said."

I stared at her, dumbfounded. I'd known Jackson was a jerk but I'd never heard of anyone being that deliberately cruel and manipulative. This was a whole new level of bullying and I couldn't believe that Nori had been trying to deal with it on her own for all this time.

"The people who are really your friends will believe you," Mara said quietly.

"Yeah, well, there haven't been too many people sticking up for me so far." Nori looked down at her plate and sniffled.

"But that's because you didn't tell us what was happening,"

Rob said. "Only *his* friends knew about it, right? So, of course it's going to feel like everyone is against you."

"It's so embarrassing, though. I don't want everyone knowing how stupid I was to trust him. And how I can't make him stop no matter what I do. I feel, I don't know, like weak and powerless. I hate feeling like that."

"Because you're not weak," I said fiercely. "And you're not powerless. And you've got all of us standing behind you. And your mom would be your biggest defender if you told her everything. That kid wouldn't know what hit him."

"Yeah, maybe," she said. "I don't want to talk about this anymore right now, though. I just want to eat."

We let it drop and I was at least glad that she looked a little more cheerful and was able to eat her lunch.

We were just pulling up the hill leaving town when her phone began to ping insistently again.

"Nori, just turn it off," Mara told her. "We'll be out of cell range once we get off this road anyway."

I turned around to see Nori calmly peeling the protective case off her phone. Without saying a word she rolled the window down and then threw the phone as hard as she could into the road behind us. It cracked apart, pieces flying off of it as it bounced down the road.

"Wow, that feels so much better," she said, rolling up the window again.

Rob and I exchanged a glance and Mara gave Nori a high-five.

I guessed that was one way to get Jackson out of her life, at least temporarily.

CHAPTER 17

The days flew by in a haze of sunshine, horses, and hard work. And all the while, the date for our archery clinic drew closer.

We rode all the horses every day until the ranch horses could have probably cantered the archery course in their sleep. We were able to shoot from their backs at all three gaits and were pretty confident that they could handle their new riders once the clinic started.

Ice had progressed, too. I could now walk, trot, and canter him around the pasture with ease. His balance was coming along, and he was slowly gaining strength and muscle tone.

I could shoot off of him now at the walk, too. He would have been happy enough to let me shoot off him at the trot and canter, but he had a tendency to be a little clumsy at times when something distracted him. He'd swing his head around and lose his balance and trip over his own feet.

He was calm and brave and was happy to try just about anything I suggested even if he didn't really understand. I was growing more attached to him every day and I was really hoping that Aunt Lillian would let me and Rob take him home.

Every night after our workday was done, Rob and I would ride Red and Artimax, either in the big ring at the training barn or on the network of trails that criss-crossed the property. Riding Red was still the best part of my day and making sure that I spent time with him helped eased the guilt I felt at spending time with so many different horses.

"You're always my best boy, Red," I told him, kissing his wide forehead. He blinked at me sleepily and rubbed his nose up and down gently on my arm. I knew that he didn't mind the vacation, he was happy here and he loved spending the day hanging out with his friends in the sun and working with me or trail riding in the evenings. But I still couldn't shake the thought that I was neglecting him a little.

As the days before the clinic flew past, I felt both more confident and more nervous than I had before. Everything that we could think of was organized. Aunt Lillian`s check lists were completed one by one. The ring was ready, the targets were ready, even that silly horse on wheels was ready. The food had been bought and meal plans organized, the rooms were ready for anyone who was sleeping in the main house or the bunk house and a flat area down by the barn had been mown down for those who would be camping in tents.

A row of green portable toilets had been set up by the ring to accommodate all the new guests, and hand washing and snack stations had been set up outside the barn, too.

The horses were solid and not afraid of any of the archery equipment and Rob, Nori, and I were pretty confident we wouldn't embarrass ourselves at the clinic.

CHAPTER 18

It wasn't until we were a few weeks in that there was any more mention of Rob's new project horse.

We'd been cooling off on the indoor bleachers watching Folly's ride late one afternoon after all our work was done. Liza's lessons had started early that morning so she hadn't been able to ride her own horses until the afternoon. Which was good timing for us because we were actually in time to watch.

"Hey, you two," she called as soon as she'd brought Folly down to a loose-reined walk. "I've been meaning to catch up with you."

She ambled over, Folly pausing to snort and itch her nose on one leg and then shake all over like a dog before continuing on.

"I feel like I've been neglecting you guys," she said, laughing. "You haven't been getting many lessons."

"We're keeping busy," Rob said, although I knew that as much as he was enjoying the ranch horse project, he would love to have more of a dressage focus, too.

"Yes, I know. I have a mare that I want you to look at, Rob. She's out on pasture right now, but I've been keeping my eye on her and I'd really like how she's developing. She's just turned four and she still has some growing to do. There are a few others out there to look at as well. But"—she turned to me with her eyebrows raised—"if you're only taking two then I wasn't sure where Astrid's big white friend fits into the picture."

"I'm not sure either, actually," I said, glancing at Rob. "Hilary's going to kill me if I try and bring home another horse to our farm. Nori's already dreaming up some scheme to take all the ranch horses back to the island with us so they don't get sent to auction."

"Hmm, lots to think about," Liza said, looking back and forth between us. "Even though you don't believe in yourself as much as you should, Astrid, you're actually very good with the young horses. You're a solid rider and you don't demand anything that they can't give. I think they instinctually trust you. These aren't the type of horses to buck or be mean. You and Rob would make a good team in bringing them along."

"See, I told you so," Rob said, bumping my arm with his elbow.

"So, you think I should take Ice home for myself and Rob should get his own projects?"

"I actually think you should work together. You have different skill sets to bring to the table. You'd be better getting the young horses going and Rob could put the finishing touches on them and get them exposure since you aren't in love with showing."

"I don't mind showing," I said quickly.

"I know. But you don't *love* it like Rob does."

I turned to look at Rob, realizing suddenly that it was true. I'd never really thought about that part of his life but, even though his schedule was even busier than mine, he really did make an effort to plan entire seasons of showing, for multiple horses in multiple disciplines, whereas I had enough trouble organizing myself for even one outing.

"Okay, yeah, that makes sense."

"So, if I was organizing your life, I'd say that you do the majority of the groundwork and basic conditioning work, and

Rob concentrates on finessing their skills and targeting them to the right market. That way, you could have a few more horses going at once. You could divide them up between Hilary and Rob's place. I really don't think Hilary would care as long as their board was being paid by someone. Oona would be happy to help you with the groundwork, I'm sure."

"She would," I said, "she loved helping me with Red."

"Right, well, you guys should really think about it then. These horses would sell well in your area, better than here actually, and for decent prices. I think you could make a bit of money."

"Okay, we'll think about it," Rob said slowly. "I don't want Astrid getting overwhelmed with work like last year. That was really bad. Like she was cran-ky."

"Hey, I'm pretty sure I can handle it. Besides, I'm *never* cranky." I sent him a mock glare.

"Uh-huh. Sure."

"Now that we have barn help at Hilary's place it's not so bad. And Hilary is doing so much more of her share now. I think I could try and have a project horse again."

I realized suddenly that I wasn't arguing just so that I could keep Ice around a little longer. The vision that Liza had presented stood in front of me like a tantalizing dream that hovered just outside of my reach. I loved working with the horses and with Rob every day. It was going to be hard enough leaving the ranch to go back to my old life without giving that part of it up, too.

But where does archery fit in to all this? I wondered. I didn't think I wanted to give up teaching at the range and competing, either. And I had to put at least a little effort into my school work since it was my final year and all. Would I end up spreading myself too thin again like last year?

That afternoon we rode out with Liza to one of the lower pastures, the one on the other side of the lake, to find the project horses. The two-, three-, and four-year-olds had been grouped in one large band this year and my heart sank when I saw how many there were.

"I know, it's a bit overwhelming," Liza said, "but Justin and I are moving through them at a good rate. We've sold a lot and now that there are fewer mares bred, we're starting to make a little headway. We're concentrating on the four-year-olds mostly, although Justin starts a few of the most promising younger ones, too."

She stood up in her stirrups and pointed out a well-proportioned bay mare. "That's the one I'd like you to consider, Rob. Her name is Starling. She's one of Fox's offspring. She's a good mover, she's built uphill, and she's a nice horse, although she does have her own opinions."

Rob jumped down and handed me Artimax's reins. I stayed in the saddle since the view was better from Red's back and watched Rob approach the mare.

She was very pretty. Her coat was a rich mahogany which stood out sharply against her dark legs and thick black mane and tail. She had a fine, intelligent face, and was watching Rob's approach with interest.

She sniffed his outstretched hand and then gently searched his pockets to see if he had treats. She crunched the piece of carrot that he gave her thoughtfully and let him scratch her neck, and then she turned abruptly and pushed her way to the far side of the herd, deciding firmly that Rob's visit was over.

"See?" Liza laughed "She knows what she wants. But she isn't mean at all. Feel free to walk around and see if anything else catches your eye."

While Rob immersed himself in the herd, Liza and I sat down in the long grass and caught up in a way we hadn't been able to until now. She asked me all about Hilary and Darius and about all the little details about life at Home Farm.

I told her all about how Caprice was doing, and filled her in on Oona's project-horse Pants.

"That horse sounds perfect for her," Liza said, smiling. "She deserves to have something of her own to love. It nearly broke her heart when she had to leave Furioso behind."

"She never told me what really happened in Belgium."

"Oh, it's not a secret, I suppose. I just think she doesn't like to be reminded of it. She was in this really bad relationship with one of her clients. Not at the school where she taught, but in the town where she lived. He owned some amazing horses and he was beautiful and charismatic. But he had a dark side too and could be hard on the horses when things weren't going his way, and on the people around him."

"Did he … did he hit her?" I asked, biting my lip. I thought of how suffocating it had been living in the same house as my father.

"She never said, but yes, I think so. At least a couple of times. She loved him very much in the beginning but by the end, she probably just stayed for Furioso. She couldn't stand to leave him behind and there was no way her boyfriend was going to sell him to her. Even if she could have afforded it."

"So what happened? How did she leave?"

"Things got pretty bad before she decided to leave. He didn't want her to work for the riding school anymore. He was super controlling and he only wanted her to ride his horses. So he got her fired."

"Wow, how?"

"It's a small town. He was a rich guy with connections and he basically pressured the school to let her go."

"That is awful."

"Honestly? I think they did her a favour. She'd mentioned to me that her boss was worried about her and he'd warned her about her boyfriend when she'd first started dating him. I almost think that firing her was a last-ditch attempt to get her out of that situation."

"So, what happened?"

"Well, she had a good idea what he'd done so she confronted him and he basically said her only choice was to stay with him or that he'd take it out on Furioso He sort of held the horse hostage so she'd do what he wanted."

"She didn't stay after that, did she?" I remembered that night I'd run away. I'd begged my stepmother Marion to go with me, to leave my dad, but she hadn't left, either.

"For a while. Things spiraled downward from there. He stopped her from seeing her friends or going out. The final straw was when he burned a bunch of her paintings. It had always been a toxic relationship, but she said it was at that point that she knew she was actually in danger."

"Oh my gosh, that is terrifying." I felt tears sting my eyes, remembering the beautiful paintings hanging in her house. "Please don't tell me that this story ends with him killing the horse. I don't think I can handle that."

"No, but she knew there was a chance that might happen when she left. She snuck out in the night knowing that there was a chance her boyfriend would take revenge on the creature she loved the most."

"But he didn't?"

"I don't think we'll ever know the details of what happened after she left. But Furioso is still alive and well now and competing all over Europe. He was sold to his new home a few weeks later. He was worth a lot of money after all and (boyfriend) wasn't completely stupid."

"Wow." I exhaled a shaky breath. "Oona was so brave to escape all that."

"I agree. Although, she still doesn't see it that way. She thinks she was a coward to stay at all."

"No, I know what that's like. She wasn't a coward."

"That's why I told you her story. I knew you'd understand a little."

"I know. I'm kind of worried about Nori for the same reason.

You heard part of her story at the restaurant. She was sort of going out with the nastiest little jerk. He's spent the last few months bullying her in the worst way. Or trying to."

"Yeah, it's a little hard to cyberbully someone when they don't have cell service or any access to the internet." Liza laughed and then looked serious again. "Do you think she's talked to her parents about it yet?"

"I don't think so. Not yet. But I'm worried what's going to happen when she's back at school in September. She's not going to be able to avoid the internet forever."

"Yeah, she definitely needs to get it dealt with. Well, Mara might be able to talk to her. They seem to be getting along and Mara went through a really rough patch with her parents this year. Hopefully they can open up to each other a little bit."

It was another half hour before Rob came out dreamily from the edge of the herd, an expression of contentment on his face. The bay mare trailed a few feet behind him. Her head was down and she was grazing but she'd take a bite and then walk a few steps, always keeping him in her sight.

"Can you ever imagine him working in an office?" I whispered to Liza before he'd come too close. "He belongs outside with the horses."

She grinned at me and nodded. "For that matter, so do you, Astrid. You both light up when you're outdoors. Nature is your happy place."

"You picked the bay mare, didn't you?" I called to Rob as he and his new friend made their way over.

"She's great," he said, smiling from ear to ear. "She acts standoffish but she isn't really. And I like the way she's put together. You're right, Liza. We'll work well together."

"I knew it. Did you pick anyone else out?"

"No." He shook his head. "There are a lot of good horses there, but I'm going to have to think about it a little more."

The mare, Starling, had drifted up to stand beside Rob and she reached out with her nose to nudge his arm.

Rob reached out to scratch her neck underneath the thick mane and she closed her eyes in contentment. It didn't look so much like he'd chosen her as that she'd chosen him.

CHAPTER 19

With a week left to go, everything was falling nicely into place for the clinic. We had rooms in the house made up for the two guests who had wanted luxury accommodation and had made up rooms in the bunkhouse over the broodmare barn as well. We had even mowed a flat spot near the barn for tents to be set up for those who were camping.

Stalls were ready for the six new horses that were trailering in with their riders, and our own ranch horses looked much more presentable after a few weeks of hard grooming and exercise.

We were so caught up in preparations that I hardly had time to worry about my parents' impending visit. Or about Nori being harassed by that loser Jackson. Or about the fact that Aunt Lillian kept dropping hints that she'd love me to stay at the ranch forever. My future was still an uncertain cloud hanging over me. Would it be horses or archery, or would I drop it all and go to school for something completely different? Ranch life or Island life? Sometimes the answers were completely clear to me and then it would become hazy again.

I tried to keep busy enough that I didn't have time to think but every so often, in those rare quiet moments, I caught Rob watching me as if he knew a little of the whirlwind that was going on inside my head.

It wasn't all work, though; in between taking care of the horses and doing training rides, we explored all the trails in the area and swam and stayed up late hanging out in front of the fire ring on the front lawn, roasting marshmallows so we could stuff our faces with S'mores and stay up talking every night until the mosquitos drove us indoors.

So far it had been one of the best summers I could remember having.

CHAPTER 20

When the day came for Laszlo Belko to finally arrive, the morning was crisp and clear with a dazzling blue sky overhead. Which meant that it would most likely be unbearably scorching by lunchtime.

Mr. Belko was coming a day ahead of everyone else to get settled in, shake off the jet-lag, and make sure all of our preparations were perfect. The rest of the participants would start arriving the next day. They would have a chance to meet each other, get to know the ranch and settle the horses, and then the first lesson would begin that evening.

Aunt Lillian was already up and dressed by the time I made it to the kitchen, still foggy with sleep and heading to the coffee pot like a zombie.

"I should be back in a couple of hours, Astrid. There are platters of snacks in the fridge so please don't eat those until we arrive. I'll call you if we're going to be late. Keep an eye on Jake and make sure he goes outside again in a couple of hours. He's not able to hold his bladder like he used to, and he won't remember to ask to go out until it's too late. Keep the house nice and tidy, and let's make sure the barn is in good order. We want to make a good first impression. From what I've heard, he's very exacting."

I nodded blearily. "Okay, we will. See you soon."

I yawned and sat down at the table with my coffee clutched between my hands, waiting for the sleep to clear from my head. We'd stayed up extra late the night before, too excited about the upcoming clinic to sleep and it had been well past midnight by the time we made it inside. It had been fun at the time but now I was solidly regretting it.

There was no sign of Nori or Rob, so I grabbed an apple from the bowl on the counter and shuffled to the front door to find my boots. I slid them on my bare feet ignoring the bits of hay and sand in the bottom that were rough against my toes.

The truck started up on the second try and I eased the rattling vehicle down the shortcut to the barn.

The horses whickered sleepily when I arrived. I threw them all hay and then went into the feed room to mix up their grain, snapping my apple core in two and throwing the pieces into Red's and Ice's buckets.

I didn't linger very long like I usually did. My plan was to just feed quickly and then go back to the house to make everyone blueberry pancakes. We'd arranged it last night and had invited Mara and Casey for breakfast too, so I didn't have much time.

When I got back to house there were voices in the kitchen and already the smell of food cooking wafted out to me.

"Come on, Astrid, we started without you," Olive squealed in her high-pitched voice. "Surprise. We made crepes!"

I paused at the edge of the kitchen where it seemed that every bowl and pan in the house had been used and then dumped in the sink. Thin pancakes, bacon, eggs, and sausages were sizzling on the stove. A fresh pot of coffee was brewing and Casey was using the electric mixer to froth up some whipped cream. Some sort of fragrant, fruity concoction bubbled away in a giant saucepan on the stove spattering pinkish liquid in a halo around it on the stovetop.

"Ah, sorry, it's a bit of a mess." Nori flashed me a guilty smile. "But I'm sure it will taste great."

"Hey," Casey said, glancing up. Her glasses were flecked with little bits of whipped cream. "Pancakes are too boring. Crepes just elevate the morning, don't you think?"

"Wow," I said, feeling a little horrified at the mess.

"Don't worry, we have lots of time to clean up," Nori said, waving a spoonful of batter through the air. A sticky blueberry plopped onto the floor where Jake was sprawled out and he snapped it up eagerly, licking the floor with his long pink tongue.

"Has he been outside again yet?" I asked.

"Um, I don't think so," Mara said. "He hasn't left the kitchen since we've been here. Rob's in the shower so we started on breakfast. It shouldn't be too much longer."

"Well, it smells great." My stomach growled and I decided to just enjoy the good breakfast and worry about the mess later. I would put Jake out again after we ate.

"Hey, you're back." Rob came up behind me and draped an arm over my shoulder. "Wow, that is quite the spread, you guys. Did you use every single dish in the house?"

"Oh, stop complaining, grandpa," Nori said, sliding a finished crepe onto the waiting stack. "Just eat. We'll clean up afterwards."

He laughed in my ear, kissed the back of my neck and sauntered to the table.

"I made a peach filling and some whipped cream for the crepes," Casey said, "and there is maple syrup on the table if you need it."

"And bacon," Mara said, "and some eggs. And sausages. We might have made a little much."

"Don't worry," I reassured her. "We can always take the leftovers down to Justin and Liza. It looks great, you guys. Crepes are actually one of my favourite foods."

That was a little misleading since I pretty much loved *all* food, but the smell of the peach filling really was amazing.

My taste buds practically did a little skip of joy when I took my first bite.

"Holy cow, Casey, this is delicious. Did you make these yourself?"

"It's Dad's recipe. He used to make them for us all the time when he wasn't so busy. He makes a blueberry one to die for, too."

We were in the middle of stuffing our faces, listening to Lincoln tell us some funny thing that happened at his last archery competition when Jake began to whine from his spot under the table and then gave a loud booming bark.

"What is it, boy?" I started to say but just then Olive gave a little startled shriek and Jake woofed again, scrambling to get up so that his head banged against the table, rattling my coffee cup hard enough that it sloshed coffee everywhere.

"There's a weird man in the house," Ollie said as Jake scrabbled toward the door, his claws slipping on the wooden floor.

"Jake, wait," I ordered, because he could be snappy with strangers sometimes.

I pushed back my chair just as an impossibly tall, stern-faced man appeared in the kitchen doorway. He surveyed the room as if he owned it, taking in our stunned faces, our half-eaten breakfast, the piles of messy dishes and the spatters of sauce and bacon grease everywhere.

I managed to grab Jake's collar before he could lunge at the man and it was at that moment that I realized that I had definitely waited too long to let the dog out this morning, because in his excitement he lost control of his bladder all over the kitchen floor.

"Oh, Jake. Oh, I'm so sorry," I said, not sure if I was talking to the dog or to the horrified man in front of me. A man whose sharp-planed face and grey beard was suddenly very familiar.

Laszlo Belko had arrived.

CHAPTER 21

I dragged Jake outside, my cheeks flaming with mortification. Why was Mr. Belko here so early? And without Aunt Lillian? He must have thought he'd walked into a complete madhouse. Maybe he'd refuse to teach us.

A strange car sat outside in the parking lot so clearly our new instructor had driven himself rather than be picked up at the airport. Somehow their wires had been crossed.

"It's not your fault," I told Jake, helping him down the stairs to the lawn, "but you'll have to stay out here for a while. Good boy."

I crept back inside, going first to the big hall closet to grab a bucket and a mop, not looking forward to the either the clean-up job or the explanation and apology ahead of me. But by the time I got to the kitchen, I found that the worst of the mess had already been toweled up and to my shock, Laszlo was now sitting at the table with a plate full of breakfast in front of him and Nori was pouring him a cup of coffee.

He didn't look stern at all now. He smiled as he dug into his crepes.

I listened in astonishment as I filled the mop bucket with sudsy water and got to work at cleaning the floor.

"You looked so scary when you first came in," Olive was saying excitedly. She'd parked herself right next to his chair and was staring at his face in fascination. "I thought you were a vampire."

"Like this?" he said, showing her his human fangs and making a little vampire hiss.

"Yes," she squealed, breaking into laughter. "But you're nice."

"Well, I'm glad you think so. I'd rather have this nice breakfast than eat little children any day."

"You need to meet my horse, Salsa. I think she'd make a great archery horse, but my dad says I'm not allowed to even try it until I'm older, which is stupid. Don't you think that's stupid?"

"Yes, a little," he said, nodding at her seriously. "There are many children, even smaller than you, who compete at mounted archery events. It is not much more dangerous than any other horse sport."

"That's what I told him—" Olive began.

"Let him eat his breakfast in peace, Ollie," Casey said, glaring meaningfully at her sister. "I think we've traumatized him enough."

By the time a tired and very irritated Aunt Lillian made it back to the ranch, we'd already shown Laszlo the barns and our homemade archery course with targets. He'd met, and approved of, our team of horses, and we'd pulled out our fake barrel horse, Fred, for him to look at, too.

"So it seems you arrived safely on your own," she said. But her gritted expression softened a little when he took her hand and kissed it.

"I apologize for the misunderstanding. You've done a wonderful job setting up your beautiful facility for the clinic. I trust everything will go smoothly in your capable hands."

"Hmm," was all she said but you could tell she'd already halfway forgiven him.

Later that day, Mr. Belko watched as we worked the horses through the course. I'd been a little nervous to ride for him. He'd taught people at the international level all over the world and I wondered how we'd stack up. As mounted-archers, we were basically entirely self-taught. Darius had helped us get started in the beginning but Nori, Rob, and I had pretty much learned by watching videos online and just practicing until our arrows could hit the target the majority of the time.

I glanced over at Laszlo now and again, but his expression was unreadable. He just stood there with his arms crossed over his chest, nodding or frowning every now and then.

"Good, good," he said when we were all done. "These horses will work nicely. Who is this handsome fellow here?"

"This is my horse, Red," I said, reaching down to scratch my favourite chestnut neck.

"I like him very much. I have a potential client looking for a good, experienced horse. Is he for sale?"

"No," I said quickly, glancing around to make sure Aunt Lillian wasn't anywhere nearby. Technically, Red was my horse to borrow from her forever, but there was always the slight chance that she wouldn't turn down a generous cash offer. "Never."

"Fair enough." He laughed. "I wouldn't sell him, either. You ride and shoot very well, my dear. I can tell you've done this a lot."

"All the time. We built our own course at home. Rob and Nori and I shoot a couple times a week, at least, and then Nori and I take archery lessons at the range, too."

"Well, I won't insult you by telling you you're a natural then, since you clearly work so hard at it."

"Astrid *is* a natural," Nori said quickly. "Before her accident she was going to shoot at the Olympics and everything."

"Not quite," I said quickly. "That was a dream, Nori. A goal. But I was still a long way away from getting there."

"That's not what Earl told me," Nori said frowning. "He's your coach, he should know."

"Anyway," Rob interrupted. "Would you like to see the range now?"

Nori shot him a dark look but let it go.

CHAPTER 22

That night we were so exhausted that we practically fell into bed right after doing night-check on the horses.

My alarm went off at the crack of dawn and I sat up abruptly, feeling a shiver of excitement ripple down my spine. This was it. All the hard work we'd done had led up to this exact moment.

I jumped out of bed and threw on the clothes that I'd set out the night before. Thankfully I'd thought to do laundry a few days before so I actually had a clean pair of jeans and a nice polo shirt that didn't have holes or stains on it.

I took extra time with my hair and put on a little make-up, it felt like a horse-show morning for some reason.

Most of the riders who were coming from out of town were driving themselves. There were just a couple of people to pick up at the bus stop in Triple Hills, and Justin had agreed to meet the lone afternoon bus when it got into town.

When the first vehicle crunched up the gravel driveway, Rob and I shot each other a look of excitement and got up at the same time to peer out the front window.

"That looks fancy," Rob said, raising his eyebrows. "That's a Hummer."

It looked like an oversized cross between an SUV and an armoured car to me. The paint was a metallic blue with silver flecks and the windows were all darkly tinted so we couldn't see who was inside. I could see a large mounted archery decal on the rear side window, though.

"Who do you think it is?" Nori asked, peering down at her list.

A young guy who didn't look older than his early twenties pushed open the door and sprang lightly to the ground. He stood and stretched and surveyed the log house with an air of indifference.

"Well, don't just stand there staring," Aunt Lillian said, coming up behind us. "Go say hello and bring him inside. Don't forget to offer to carry his things. You'll have to learn to be better hosts than that."

"Well, *I'm* not a host. I don't even like people," Nori said quickly, disappearing back to the kitchen.

"That leaves us, I guess."

Rob and I put on our best smiles and went outside.

"Hey there," Rob said, "are you here for the clinic?"

The boy fixed on a smile to match ours and stepped forward. "Austin Cooper. The third. Good to meet you." He shook both of our hands with an extra hard squeeze when we introduced ourselves and grinned his toothy smile at us, but his eyes stayed cold and remote. He shifted his gaze restlessly between us and then back to the house and then the woods, never quite settling on anything.

"Well, come on inside," I said. "Um, can we help carry your things?"

"Nope, I travel light and I'll keep my bows locked in the Hummer for safekeeping. I hope there's a good horse for me. My guy got hurt a couple of months ago and I haven't found a replacement yet. Laszlo probably told you about me already. He's seen videos of my riding and knows I've won a bunch of championships and everything."

"Er, he did say he knew someone looking for a horse to buy," I said slowly. "Maybe he meant you."

"Yep, it's not as easy as you'd think. It takes forever to train a new horse to go the way you'd like and the good ones are hardly ever for sale. I've looked at a few but they were all dogs."

"Dogs?" I asked, confused.

"You know. Worthless. Only good for canning."

Rob and I exchanged a silent, wide-eyed look as we led him into the house.

Luckily, Aunt Lillian took over from us at the front door. She fussed around making sure Austin had been fed and that his room was comfortable enough.

Thankfully it was Lincoln and Ally who showed up next. They were staying in the bunk house and we hurried over to show them where to put their things while Austin was being plied with lunch by Aunt Lillian.

One by one the other riders and their horses showed up, and it was complete chaos until well after lunch.

There were only two people, Austin and a nice, quiet woman named Riley, staying in the main house with us. That was the most expensive option and Aunt Lillian had billed it as Luxury Accommodation. Most of the rest of the participants were staying in the bunkhouse over the broodmare barn with Mara. And there were two older couples who already knew each other who had brought their own oversized canvas tents to stay in.

The arrival of six new horses caused quite a bit of excitement in the barn and it took a while to settle everybody down.

It was interesting to see how different the horses all were. Riley, who it turned out had done quite a bit of competing already, had a beautiful little chestnut Arabian mare named Cashmere who had huge, intelligent eyes and a permanently startled expression.

One of the people camping out in the tents, a nice guy named

Todd, had an Arabian too, but it seemed much more laid back than Cashmere.

"Yeah, Duster is my endurance horse, too," Todd told us, scratching the little bay's neck affectionately. "So he's seen a lot. He's a solid horse and I think he'll like archery."

Todd's much younger wife Jessie had brought her Clydesdale cross, Locket, who towered over the other horses as he sauntered through the barn to his stall.

There was beautiful grey Thoroughbred named Limerick who was built like an elegant dressage horse. He was owned by a quiet young guy named John who seemed nice but didn't say much.

Bruce and Isabelle were the other couple camping out in a tent. They'd brought Bruce's prancy little Appaloosa, Cobblestone, and Isabelle had a golden Halflinger named Pogo that seemed overwhelmed by the whole situation and continued to pace her stall anxiously long after the other horses had settled down.

It wasn't until well after lunch that everyone had been settled in their accommodations for the next week, the horses were relaxing in their stalls and the nervous, excited chatter had died down into a more easy, relaxed pace.

Aunt Lillian bustled around making sure that everyone was happy, fed, and that they'd all been introduced properly to Mr. Belko.

Later that afternoon, the first lesson began. There were no horses involved; it was just us standing on foot in the cool air of the range, shooting at targets one by one while Mr. Belko assessed our form and skills.

It was such a strange mix of people that I wondered how he'd ever sort us into groups. There were a few people who actually had experience with both horses and archery, but there were others who only had horse experience and had barely even shot before, and some, like Lincoln and Ally, who were good archers but had never been around horses. And then, of course, some of the horses had never been exposed to archery, either. I did not envy Laszlo having to figure out how to teach everyone at once.

That night, when everyone was sitting around chatting after dinner at the house, I managed to slip away unnoticed to the barn. I wasn't used to all that noise and all those people, and I desperately wanted some quiet time. I tried to catch Rob's eye to tell him where I was going but he was caught up in conversation with two of the other guys in the group so I left him to it and headed out alone.

"Hey guys," I whispered, relishing the silence overlaid with just the gentle sound of them chewing their dinner.

The new horses were settling in fine and did not seem at all disturbed by their strange surroundings.

I took in a deep breath and leaned against the wall, content just to listen to them for a few minutes before I grabbed my brushes from the tack room.

"Are you the best boy, Red?" I asked him as he shuffled through the knee-deep straw toward me, sniffing at my pockets until he found the carrot he knew I'd smuggled him. I leaned my forehead against his neck, loving the solid warmth of him against my skin.

He went back to his hay while I brushed him, and I took my time even though he was pretty clean. I worked the curry comb in deep circles across his coat, massaging his muscles and working up the loose hair and dirt. He leaned into the pressure when I reached his withers, tilting his neck a little to the side as I dug into his shoulders.

The air was still hot even though it was after dinner and instead of heading for the ring, I made for the woods, following the trail that led beside the river. Red strode along on a loose rein, his head bobbing and his mane bouncing up and down gently on his neck as he marched down the pathway. His ears were pricked with excitement and I wondered if it was all the new horses arriving that had put a little extra briskness in his step.

When I got back I was dismayed to see that Austin was standing alone in the barn aisle, leaning over Ice's stall door. He looked up as I came in and flashed me a toothy smile.

"Nice horse," he said, and I couldn't tell whether he was talking about Red or Ice. Either way, I felt my hackles start to raise protectively.

"Um, thanks." I jumped to the ground and the busied myself running up my stirrups.

"I prefer Thoroughbreds usually, but these Quarterhorses are decent enough. Your aunt said she had quite a few for sale."

"She does," I said, forcing myself to be polite. After all he was a paying customer. "There are some seasoned ranch horses for sale or a whole training barn full of up and coming prospects. I could get Justin to show you what we have available if you like."

"Yeah, that would be great. What about this one?"

I gulped and tried not let my anger show as he waved a hand idly at Ice.

"He's just a baby. He's really only had a few weeks under saddle and he's barely cantering. You probably want something a little further along in training."

"I don't know. This whole summer is pretty much blown competition-wise anyway. Iggy pulled a ligament and it's going to take at least six months to a year to get him fixed. He's going to be out on pasture getting fat for a while."

"Oh, you're keeping him?" I asked, thinking that maybe Austin wasn't as horrible as I'd thought if he'd spend the time and money rehabbing an injured horse.

"Might as well." He shrugged and looked up at the ceiling, studying a pigeon rustling in the rafters. "I put a lot of money and time into getting him perfect. I don't want to throw that all away."

"Right," I said, leading Red to his stall. As we went inside Portia let out an outraged *baa* and barged into the aisle. I'd kept her locked up for the last few days since I didn't know what Mr. Belko would think about a sheep, and I didn't want her messing up our perfectly clean aisle. But she'd clearly had enough of that.

She galloped right down the aisle and out the front door, kicking up her heels when she reached the lawn.

"What the heck was that?" Austin looked at me incredulously.

"A sheep," I said with a sigh, "she's a pet. Her name is Portia. She normally lives with Red here. She's his friend."

"Weird. So would whoever bought him have to take the sheep, too?"

I froze, my fingers gripping the throatlatch I was unfastening.

"Pardon?" I asked coldly. "Red is not for sale."

"That's not what your aunt said. She said everything here is for sale for the right price."

"Yah, well, she didn't mean Red. He was my Uncle Trent's favourite horse and now he's mine."

That last part wasn't strictly true but it was close enough. I would never let Aunt Lillian sell Red. Never.

"Well, maybe she just hasn't been offered enough money yet."

"Look—" I laid a hand protectively on Red's neck.

"Okay, okay," Austin interrupted, raising his hands and giving me a little smirk. "No need to get yourself all excited. I haven't even made an offer yet. Maybe I'll look around and see if something else catches my eye."

He sauntered out without another word and I honestly had never felt so much rage or wanted to hit someone so much in my life. My hands were actually shaking as I pulled off the rest of Red's tack and put it away.

I was still in shock while I groomed him. I ran the soft bristled brush over his silky sides until he shone like copper, my mind whirling. I thought of what Oona had said before I'd left to come to the ranch. That I should buy him quick before someone else did.

It was only the sound of the rest of the participants coming back to the bunkhouse that finally shook me out of my fog.

CHAPTER 23

The next morning we brought our five ranch horses out to the make-shift ring to match them with their new riders. Laszlo Belko was already down at the far end of the grassy field assessing the riders who'd brought their own horses.

I didn't envy him as the nine riders cantered around him. Everyone was using different gear; it was a mixture of western, english, and stock horse tack, and Bruce, one of the bearded campers, had a sort of homemade leather bareback pad that he'd strapped to his fiery little Appaloosa. Some of the riders sat very still and balanced, like Rob, but others were wilder, and I winced as one of the girls sawed at her horse's mouth to get it to turn.

Mr. Belko had asked Rob, Nori, and I to do the initial matching of the ranch horses and riders, and then he would move people around as needed. After meeting everyone, we'd sat down and come up with a list.

"Here, Ally," I said, "this is Piper. She's super sweet and kind, and she'll take care of you out there. I think you'll really like her."

The black mare was already half-asleep but she opened her eyes briefly as Ally ran a hand gently down her neck.

"She's so beautiful," she said, looking at the mare with shining eyes.

"Hardly, it looks about a hundred years old," Austin muttered under his breath. But Ally was too entranced with Piper to notice him.

"And Lincoln, I think you'll like Whiskey. He's very solid and dependable."

"Perfect," Lincoln said, taking the reins by the very ends and standing just about as far away from the little Paint as he could. "Uh, good horse. Stay."

"Candace, the bay mare here is Rocket and I think you should try her out. She's forward and fun, but also very steady. And Sasha, this guy is Fenwick. He's my personal favourite."

They both looked pleased with my choices, but I think they were just excited to be riding anything at all.

"Austin, that means you'll be riding Kestrel here. She's fast and handy. She should be what you're looking for."

"Um, she's pink," Austin said, raising his eyebrows skeptically.

"She's a red roan. That's what they look like."

"Don't you have anything in a different colour?"

"No," I said, trying to keep the irritation out of my voice. "Haven't you heard the saying 'a good horse is never a bad colour'? Just try her out. I'm sure you'll like her."

I actually wasn't sure about that at all. It seemed to me that the only thing Austin really liked was himself.

Sorry, Kestrel, I thought guiltily as he led her away toward the other riders. *It's only for a week.*

Lincoln and Ally had stayed behind when everyone else left and they were both looking at me expectantly as if for directions.

"Right," I said, realizing that the two of them had zero horse experience and were going to need help every step of the way. "So you're going to hold the reins like this, and step beside their shoulder and then just start walking."

"Oooh, she's following me," Ally said in excitement. "It's working."

"Mine's broken," Lincoln said, and I turned to see him standing facing his horse. He tugged lightly on the reins and shook his head.

"Well, he can't really go forward if you're standing there blocking him," I said, trying not to laugh.

"Astrid, he's like ten times bigger than me. He can go wherever he likes."

"Yeah, but he's not a wild mustang. He's been trained not to walk over people. See, just turn in the direction you want to go and start walking."

I clucked a little under my breath to encourage a very confused Whiskey to move along and soon, we were all moving in a somewhat orderly fashion down the hill.

"Okay, how do I stop her?" Ally asked, sounding worried.

"Just stop walking. She'll stay right beside you."

Ally halted abruptly and her face lit up when Piper ambled to a stop, too.

"Wow, this is amazing. Thank you so much. I love her."

"Whooaaaa," Lincoln said, drawing the one horsey term he knew out as he turned to look at his horse and put both hands in the air like he was stopping a runaway bull. Whiskey stopped abruptly and looked at his new rider incredulously and then looked around him as if he couldn't believe what he had to deal with.

"You can be very subtle with them," I said, trying not to smile. After all, Lincoln was brand new at this. How was he supposed to know how to handle a horse? "They're very good at reading your body language so you don't have to use any big gestures or be loud or anything. He's a well-trained horse. He'll get it."

"Right," Lincoln said, patting Whiskey hesitantly on the neck a couple of times. "Good horse. Stand and stay."

"Um," I started to correct him and then just shrugged and let it go. He'd see what everyone else was doing and pick up on things eventually.

I looked up to see Laszlo watching us from across the field with a small smile on his face.

The riders who had brought their own horses had already finished their assessment by that time and had left with Nori and Rob to go on a short trail ride. Mara had stayed behind to watch Austin, Candace, and Sasha who were now trotting around the big ring while Mr. Belko watched them with his eyes narrowed and his arms crossed over his chest.

"Good," he said now and then, although it was hard to know which rider he meant. "Now canter."

I was surprised to see that, despite his cocky attitude, Austin wasn't actually a very good rider. He was sloppy in the walk and gave very little direction to Kestrel at all. He left his reins hanging, letting her guess which direction she should go in until he jerked her in the mouth when she started heading off across the field.

He bounced all over in the trot and his posting was strange; he rose very high in the air and his legs swung forward and back against her sides. Kestrel, being the superstar she was, only put her nose in the air and hollowed her back in protest, still trying her best to figure out what this strange new rider was asking.

Austin's best gait was the canter, but that was because he just locked himself in one position and stayed there. But at least that meant that he kept off Kestrel's back so she was able to move forward into a nice fluid canter.

I guess all the competitions are held at a canter or gallop so that's all he's used to, I thought, struggling not to be too judgy. Still, I had no idea how he'd managed to win all the competitions he'd bragged about. He had zero balance and I felt that if his horse stopped suddenly, he would just fly over its head. *His injured horse, Iggy, must be a saint.*

Candace and Sasha were both nice, quiet riders who took

their time to figure out how the horses needed to be ridden. I was sure that once they gained confidence in Rocket and Fenwick that they would develop some really nice partnerships.

"All right, now let's have our beginner riders over," Laszlo called after he'd sent the others off on their own trail ride with Mara. I saw Lincoln and Ally exchange panicked looks.

"Um, we won't have to do the racing in circles part, will we?" Ally asked, twisting the reins nervously between her fingers.

"No, he'll probably just ask you to walk. Maybe trot at the most."

"Okay, let's do this." Lincoln gritted his teeth like he was headed off to war and strode purposefully toward the mounting block, only turning around a few times to make sure Whiskey was inching along behind him.

They didn't get to trot until the very end of their lesson. Once I showed them how to mount up properly, and how to hold the reins, Laszlo just had them walk around him in a circle, one following the other, and then change direction a few times. Then he had them walk all the way down the make-shift chute past the targets and then loop around the field and do it again. He walked beside them, quietly asking them to make small adjustments to their position until they were both sitting quite naturally.

Even though it was all done at a snail's pace, both riders were grinning from ear to ear and you could see how proud they were. Ally kept patting Piper enthusiastically on the neck and Lincoln stopped sitting like a petrified soldier and slouched into his version of a cowboy.

Then they were allowed to do the whole thing over at a slow trot.

I was bursting with pride for them. Nobody had fallen off, or cried, and the horses had behaved themselves perfectly.

This is just like teaching archery, only better, I thought dreamily. Apparently, introducing people to horses made my heart very happy.

By the time we'd finished our own, very slow, trail ride down to the river and then back to the barn, Rob's group had put their horses away and were sitting in the aisle, eating snacks and waiting for us. Even Austin seemed to be enjoying himself; he wasn't such a pain when he wasn't talking.

"How did it go?" Rob asked, looking at me expectantly.

"Perfect," I said, beaming at Ally and Lincoln.

"Are the saddles always this hard?" Lincoln winced as he crawled off Whiskey's back and limped into the barn.

"Uh, kind of," Rob said, raising an eyebrow. Maybe we can find some padding for you."

"No, no, that's fine," Lincoln sighed. "I'll toughen up."

"Piper is just the nicest horse," Ally said dreamily. "I'm so glad I'm riding her. I've wanted to do this for so long. It's the best birthday present ever and the best part is that I get to share this with Lincoln, too. Thanks for helping us, Astrid."

"You're welcome. You both did great out there." I beamed at them, thinking again that they made the most adorable couple. And Lincoln was pretty amazing to be putting himself through all of this for Ally. Horses clearly weren't his cup of tea, but he was doing his best to have fun.

"Here, I'll help you untack." Rob moved into Whiskey's stall to show Lincoln how to take off the heavy saddle. "Everyone else is heading over to the archery range to look at the bows and get anyone who doesn't have their own stuff fitted with equipment."

"Mine was custom made for me," Austin said around a mouthful of chips. "It had to come all the way from Mongolia. It cost nearly two grand."

Was it inlaid with gold and sapphires? I thought sceptically. I had never seen a horse bow that expensive, but I supposed they were out there if you looked for them.

"Wow, that's amazing," Sasha said, looking up at him with shining eyes. His good looks had clearly blinded her to his personality. "I bought mine off eBay for like a hundred bucks. I hope Laszlo doesn't tell me it's garbage or anything."

I busied myself helping Ally get Piper untacked and then I practically had to drag her out of the stall. She wanted to keep brushing and fussing over her new friend forever.

We met everyone else at the archery range where they were already busy examining the pile of bows and equipment Laszlo had made us haul down there the night before. He had about twenty different types and styles of bows with all different weights and lengths. Plus a whole bunch of gear I didn't even recognize.

I stared at them with interest. When I'd originally bought my horse bow online, I'd known nothing and had just had to guess at what I'd wanted. I'd had no idea there were that many options out there.

"Good, you're all here," he said warmly. "Let me just start by saying that choosing a bow is a very personal thing. There are no wrong answers but there are some guidelines I can share with you. Even if you are an experienced archer in other disciplines you need to understand that the technique of shooting a horse bow is unique. The way I was taught is to shoot with a thumb release. I know that the three fingered, or the Mediterranean draw, is favoured in some schools, and is probably what most of you are more familiar with, but I can tell you that your speed and accuracy will be much better if you can use the thumb release instead. This is my personal opinion, of course; you'd probably find others who disagree."

He smiled at us broadly and we all smiled back; the room filled with laughter.

"I will teach you both techniques and you can find the one that works for you. Now, let us begin."

The next hour was one of the most interesting I'd ever spent. First of all, I'd never even heard of the thumb draw before. I'd always shot the horse bow just like I did my regular recurve bow, using my three fingers on the string. With the thumb draw, the archer sort of looped the string through their thumb and index finger. It was supposed to make for a smoother and faster release but it also looked a bit awkward.

I'd thought that I knew quite a bit about horse archery since I shot off Red all the time and played on our course in the woods. But it turned out that I didn't know very much at all about the history of the sport, or of the many different styles of bow. Or of all the different types of competitions. It seemed like almost every country in the world had a slightly different style of riding, shooting and bow construction.

The most common competition courses were the Hungarian, Korean, and Japanese style, but it turned out that the archery course we'd set up in the woods at home on the farm was more like the cross-country or Polish style. We'd just built it that way because it was fun and convenient, but apparently it was the most difficult course you could do too, which had accidentally given us a bit of an advantage when it came to more traditional competitions.

As for the bows themselves, there were dozens and dozens of different types, and even when you picked a type you liked, there were different variations of bone and wood and sinew, and then every custom bow maker would throw in slight variations and flourishes. It was actually really overwhelming.

Some of the participants had their own bows, of course, and after our lecture on fit and style, we were told to go bring ours back to the range so that Laszlo could look at them and see how well they suited us.

"Ah," he said, when he looked at my well-used fiberglass bow. "This is a good beginner bow to have in your arsenal. But now it's maybe time to move up to something else, yes?"

I looked at his array of equipment and then sighed. "I can't really afford to get anything new right now."

"Well, why don't you spend the week trying a few out so at

least you know what you like? This one here, for example, would fit you nicely. Go on, give it a try. Don't worry about trying out the thumb release yet, just shoot as you would normally."

The bow he handed me was built from layers of dark brown wood, and the grip and the middle part of the limbs were wrapped with a soft, black leather. It was simple, but very beautiful and I took it reverently, my heart beating a little more quickly.

"Go on, the pull is the same as your old bow so it shouldn't feel too different. There are its arrows. The black ones."

Maybe it should have felt the same as my own horse bow, but it was much different. It melded to my hand like it had been custom made for me. The arrows were also dark with jet black, iridescent feathers, and when I drew back and released the arrow, the string made a little humming sound that whispered like music.

The arrow flew down toward my target and buried itself soundly an inch north of the center.

"Not bad. Not bad. See how you get on with it this week."

"I would love to use it, thank you. Thank you so much."

One by one, everyone either had their own equipment approved or were matched up with borrowed things.

When Austin's turn came, he stepped forward proudly. I had to admit that his bow really was stunning. It was made of a mix of carved horn and wood and had inlayed pearl worked into the intricate designs carved down the length of it. His arrows were a gleaming silver with pearl feather fletchings.

He was a much better archer than he was a rider, thankfully, although he lacked the loose, effortless style that Rob had when he shot. His shoulders seemed braced as if we were facing an unseen enemy.

"Nice," Laszlo said quietly, "but your pull is too heavy for you. You need a lighter one for now."

"Lighter pull?" Austin said incredulously. "No way. This is what I always shoot at. It's fine."

"You struggle," Mr. Belko said simply, "when there is no need to struggle. At the end of a meet, your arms are like, ah, wet noodles, are they not?"

"No," Austin scowled at the floor. "I mean, I'm sore sometimes, but who isn't?"

"Well, suit yourself. Perhaps you could do me a favour though, and try a couple of these bows as well. You might like this one, she's a personal favourite."

He brought out a curved, bright red bow with a cream-coloured leather wrap around the hand grip. It too was made of a mixture of horn and wood, although it wasn't nearly as fancy as Austin's own.

"I've won competitions all over the world with this one," Laszlo said quietly.

The skepticism on Austin's face turned into interest as he carefully put his own bow aside and took hold of the new one. His eyes flickered a little as he tested the weight and balance of it. The arrows were a matching cream and red colour and he rolled one in his fingers a few times before nocking it swiftly and sending it flying effortlessly across the room.

"All right," he said, a smile flickering across his lips. "You're right, I do like it. How much do you want for it?"

"Oh, it's not for sale. But you can borrow it for the week and I can tell you the name of the bowyer who designed it. You could have a similar one made quite easily."

"Well, um, thanks," Austin said a bit awkwardly. Saying thank you probably wasn't something that came naturally to him.

"All right, everyone, we will break for lunch time now that you have your equipment and your horses sorted out. This afternoon I will sort you into your groups and we will have a lesson in shooting on the ground first and then from the barrel horse."

"Shooting horse?" Ally asked. "What's that?"

"Well, you shall see after lunch. I promise he will not bite or buck."

Everyone carefully put their gear away and then made their way up to the house, chattering and laughing. Rob put his arm companionably around my shoulders and I leaned into him happily, very glad that we'd decided to come up to the ranch in the first place. This was more fun than I'd had in a long time.

Aunt Lillian had lunch prepared already and we gorged on chili and cheese buns, salad, and roasted corn and mashed potatoes. It was all delicious and there was not one complaint, not even from Austin.

There was a two-hour long break after lunch and everyone drifted off to do their own things for a little while. I debated whether or not to take Ice out and work with him since I wouldn't have that much chance that evening, but in the end I was too tired and instead, Rob and I stretched out under the shade of a towering pine on the front lawn, my head pillowed on his chest. I had a book in my hands, but I was too sleepy to read and instead, I stared up dreamily at the gently waving pines overhead.

My eyes drifted shut as I was lulled into a drifting half-sleep by Rob's steady breathing and the needles in the trees rustling together. For some reason, I saw the image of the new bow that Laszlo had leant me and then of Red and Ice standing all tacked up side by side, their ears pricked as they watched me. Then I saw a crowd of people out in a wide, green field. It was some sort of competition. But instead of feeling nervous or excited, a feeling of peace settled over me.

I woke up abruptly.

"You were smiling in your sleep," Rob said, reaching out and gently pulling my hair.

"It was a good dream." I sat up and stretched. "I was surrounded by horses."

"Sounds about right." I could hear the smile in his voice.

"Would you really be okay if I brought Ice home as a project horse. I don't even know how that would work out money-wise if we're both putting hours into him."

"Go for it. We'll figure it out. I kind of like Nori's idea about taking one or two of the ranch horses instead of more young horses. They need help more than the young ones do. And they're already well-trained. They just need to be polished up. Lots of people are looking for good-mannered trail horses. And most of them aren't *that* old."

"That's a great idea. I don't like the thought of them going to auction, either. Even if Aunt Lillian insists that it's a high-class auction, I still would hate for them to end up getting into the wrong hands or going for meat somehow."

"Well, I have two spaces at my house. I'm going to take Starling home, for sure. If you can keep Ice at Hilary's, then there's a spot for one more at my house."

"There's that whole upper area across from the sheep field at Hilary's, too," I said thoughtfully. "Maybe we could build paddocks and a few shelters there. That way we could fit in a few more of the ranch horses. We still wouldn't be able to bring them all, but it would be something anyway."

"We should talk to Nori too and see how much she work she would want to help out with. We couldn't really do it without help."

We drifted off into our own thoughts, each wondering what the future would bring.

CHAPTER 24

"We will now divide ourselves into two groups," Laszlo said. "Some of you are familiar with archery, some of you are competent riders, and some of you are blessed enough to be skilled in both."

He smiled around the room and everyone laughed.

"Ally and Lincoln, you have the least horse experience so we will put you in a group together. Isabelle, Jessie, John, and Riley, your horses have not had any archery experience so we will put you in this group too so that we can move at their pace. I'll have Astrid join this group to help out and for demonstrations."

"Austin, Rob, Bruce, Todd, Mara, Nori, Sasha, and Candace all have enough familiarity with both horse and archery that we're going to group you together. Sometimes both groups will merge and learn together as a unit. We are all a team here and I trust you will all progress quickly. When we have the final competition at the end of this clinic, we will make each team a mixture of experienced and novice participants. Are there any questions?"

Nobody seemed to mind their groupings; when I looked around, everyone appeared happy and there wasn't any grumbling. Not even from Austin.

"Now we will have a fun lesson for everyone together. Even the experienced riders will get to try out our contraption. Working on form without risking your horse is a benefit to everyone."

"What is that thing?" Austin said a few minutes later, looking skeptically at our barrel horse.

I thought it looked pretty good. We'd attached a metal barrel to the wooden trailer as per our instructions and had made a sort of head and neck for it out of wood and had even made it a tail. We'd painted the whole thing brown so it looked roughly like a horse and had finished it off by bolting an ancient western saddle to it.

We'd hooked it up to the back of my truck, which chugged and sputtered alarmingly where it was idling at the beginning of our archery course. Maybe we should have picked a fancier vehicle because more than one person looked a little concerned for their safety.

"Whose up first?" Justin said, poking his head out the window and grinning. He'd been waiting for this moment for a while. "And somebody had better be taking pictures."

"I'll go," Nori said, grabbing her bow.

"Good," Laszlo said. "Show them how it's done."

We could hear Nori laughing hysterically as she bounced her way all the way around the course. It was probably way bumpier than riding on an actual horse but she still managed to hit most of the targets.

"That. Was. Amazing," she said, grinning as she flung herself out of the saddle. "Who's up next?"

There were no shortage of volunteers. And once everyone had had a turn, most people wanted to try it over and over. Justin drove slowly for those who didn't have any riding experience, but for anyone who wasn't afraid of speed he shot off across the field, only slowing down at the corners. Everyone loved it.

"This is better than a real horse," Lincoln said happily. "I'd way prefer to ride something that doesn't have its own opinions."

"No way." Ally raised her eyebrows. "The fact that horses have their own thoughts and feelings is the best part. You have to be friends with them so that they'll want to work with you. You can't force them."

"Sure you can," Austin said casually, sounding a little like a psychopath. Then he caught Sasha's startled look and quickly corrected himself. "But, I agree. It is better to be friends with them first."

He smiled around the room a little unconvincingly.

I'd thought that the barrel horse contraption had been a little silly at first, but it actually gave everyone quite a bit more confidence and a taste for speed, and Laszlo said that's how we'd start off all our morning lessons each day. We'd shoot in the range first, then take a spin on the metal horse, and then in the afternoon we'd practice on our real horses.

The riders who'd brought their own horses also had to do extra ground work lessons once a day so that their mounts were one hundred percent confident with shooting. Isabelle's little golden Halflinger mare Pogo needed lots of extra time because she shivered and shook every time the arrow left the bow.

"You must work with her from the ground every chance you get," Laszlo told her. "Three, four, five times a day. Just a few minutes here and there will make a world of difference."

I actually didn't envy some of the people who'd brought their own horses. Having to train themselves and their horses at the same time was really hard and it took a lot of time. The students who'd rented the ranch horses had a huge advantage because they only had to worry about themselves and not their mounts.

The week sped by way faster than I wanted it to. Every day we worked hard from morning until night, only stopping to eat and do our chores. I fell into bed exhausted but happy every night, too tired to think about my parents impending visit.

Marion had called once to let us now that baby Aurora continued to grow stronger and healthier, and that the doctor said she'd definitely be ready for her trip to the coast.

Austin continued to prowl around looking for his next archery horse. He and Kestrel were working together well by then, but he didn't like her colour and he kept moaning about how much better he'd be doing if he had his old horse, Iggy, with him at camp.

"She's too old," he complained. "All these ranch horses are. I need something younger, with some spark. Like Iggy has."

He had made sure to closely watch all the riders who had brought their own horses and to ask both Riley and Bruce if their horses were for sale.

"It's not about getting a horse that's already perfectly finished," Riley had told him. "You should just find a horse whose temperament you get along with best, who has a good mind and whose gaits you like, and then train him yourself. It doesn't take that long to get them ready for their first competitions and training them yourself builds that relationship of trust that you need to have with your horse."

"I did that already with Iggy," Austin said. "I just want a trained horse that does what its told this time."

Riley just shook her head and led Cashmere away.

The next morning, Aunt Lillian approached me with a nervous look on her face.

"Astrid, could you come talk to me for a moment. I have something to run past you."

She looked so anxious that I immediately thought it must be about Marion and the baby.

"Did something happen? Is everyone okay?"

"Yes, yes, of course. Everything is fine. It's just that I wanted to talk to you about Red."

I froze, my heart suddenly seizing in my chest as I saw where this was going.

"He's not for sale," I blurted out, wiping my sweating palms on my breeches. "Whatever he's offered you, I will find the money to match it. I will find a job. I will do whatever it takes. Just please don't sell Red to Austin. I can't lose him. He's my—" My throat clogged suddenly with tears.

"Okay, okay, calm down. Just breathe." My aunt laid a hand on my shoulder. "I'm not selling Red without your permission, Astrid. I just wanted to talk to you about it."

I took a few deep shuddering breaths and felt the panic gradually recede.

"You're right, Austin made me a very good offer. I know that you've been getting along very well with that young horse, Ice. I was going to say that you could have Ice instead if you wanted to sell Red. You've put all the work into that horse so Ice would be your payment for all the care you've put into training Red. I meant to tell you how impressed I am of how far he's come. He's like a completely different horse."

My mind whirled. Ice would come home not as a project horse to be sold; he would be my very own that nobody could ever take away from me. But Red ….

"No," I shook my head. "I can't do it. Red is everything to me. I love Ice, but Red has been my best friend right from the beginning. I could never do that to him."

"Horses are sold all the time, Astrid. He would adapt just fine to a new home. And Austin has a nice farm and would give him the best of care."

"No," I said again. "Never. How much do you want for him? I can figure out a way to give you the money. I'll match whatever Austin offered you."

She studied my face for a moment and then took my hand with a sigh.

"You don't have to pay me anything, Astrid. You just keep riding him like you have been. I'll tell Austin to keep looking."

She hugged me but I was still too upset to respond. Somehow

her answer didn't feel like enough. There was a question in there somewhere. Like maybe if an even bigger offer came along that she would cave in and sell him, whether I agreed or not.

Oona was right, I thought dully, *I have to find a way to buy him.*

Austin caught me a few hours later at the barn as I was putting Ice away and he wasn't happy.

"I made an incredible offer on that horse," he said, scanning the aisle to make sure we were alone. "And your aunt turned me down."

"Red is not for sale," I said firmly. "There are about a billion horses in the world that you can buy. Pick another one."

"I don't like people telling me no," Austin said, sounding about two years old. He narrowed his eyes at me and took a step forward.

I heard a burst of laughter from one of the stalls and Bruce poked his bearded head out, staring at Austin with an incredulous expression.

"Better get used to it, Austin," he called down the aisle. "There is going to be a lot of *no* in your future if you keep acting like that."

Austin blushed furiously and turned away.

"Better change your mind," he said over his shoulder to me, "or you'll regret it."

CHAPTER 25

On Thursday night the lower half of the ranch began to transform itself into a medieval paradise.

Multi-coloured tents popped up in all directions and people dressed in everything from jeans to elaborate dresses or armour swarmed everywhere, hanging banners, building the wooden castle façade, and setting up the little village.

Many of the tents became mock storefronts that sold everything from baked goods, home-brewed honey mead, leather supplies, carved wooden toys, musical instruments, dresses and other sewn things, and even a homemade candy seller.

The whole row of tents smelled heavenly; a mixture of fresh baked bread, leather, and sugar filled the air and kept our noses sniffing appreciatively.

Best of all was when the huge trailer pulling ten heavy horses lugged down the driveway. We watched in excitement as the big drafts thudded down the metal ramp. Each of their heavily feathered feet were the size of my head and many of them must have stood well above seventeen hands high. They all looked very calm and gentle, though. And they must have been used to doing festivals like these because they didn't even blink at the tents, costumes, or people practicing sword-work nearby.

One of the biggest tents had been set up with a series of long tables for the nightly feasts and Aunt Lillian had given them permission to dig a big fire pit that was filled with coals and a wooden scaffold that would be used to roast a whole pig on Saturday night. Something I would do my best to avoid.

There were still regular lessons happening in the indoor arena and you could see the surprise and then delight on the faces of the regular parents and students who pulled up in front of the barn.

Word had spread in the area and a regular parade of curious locals showed up too just to check things out. The air was thick with excitement and we grew more and more eager for our archery competition and demonstration.

The plan was to split us into two teams, each a mixture of beginner to advanced riders and archers. We would stage a mock competition that would serve to introduce people to the sport and for us to get a taste of what real competition would look like. Other than Austin, Bruce, and Candace, none of us had competed before. We would shoot all three days, with the Friday being a rehearsal of sorts since there probably wouldn't be very many people.

There would be a real trophy and some sort of prize at the end though, for the winning team.

On Thursday night, Laszlo presented us our costumes to wear, which were just rough-linen short tunics in cream or blue. They were basically roomy long shirts that were meant to be tied with a matching cloth belt. They went on over our regular clothes but would make us fit in with the rest of the festival folk and would show the spectators which team we were on.

Now we were getting really excited. Ally had her mom bring a whole bunch of coloured yarns so we could decorate the horse's manes and tails with braids if we wanted, and we spent Friday morning making them all look fancy.

"I'm so glad I'm on your team," Ally said. "I'm so nervous to have people watching me."

"Nerves are pretty normal for everyone," I told her. "Just do your best. This is all just for fun and it's not like you're really going to let us down or anything if you don't do well. We'll be cheering you on no matter what. This is about you and Piper showing off all the hard work you've done this week."

"Last night I dreamt that I didn't hit a single target. It was mortifying."

"Well, that's not going to happen today. Just take your time, go slow, and remember to breathe."

"Right. The breathing thing, I forget that sometimes."

"And, most importantly, have fun." I smiled at her and, after a moment, she smiled back and then reached over to hug Piper's neck affectionately.

"Do you think I could ride her again after the camp is over? I'd like to learn how to ride properly."

"Like, do you mean take lessons on her?"

"Yeah. My mom is working full time now so she thought maybe we could afford to have me take some lessons. Maybe I could just keep riding Piper."

"Um," I hesitated. Not wanting to say that Piper was probably destined for the auction block after this week. "She isn't actually part of their school horse string. Yet. But I can check with Liza and my aunt to see if maybe you could do that. I really don't see why not."

"Oh good, thanks, Astrid. She's such a great horse."

CHAPTER 26

Friday morning came with a little breeze in the air and I said a thankful prayer to the weather gods. Our event started at eleven o clock and, with any luck, it wouldn't be roasting by the time we were done.

The jousting would be held after lunch and I felt bad for all those riders galloping around in heavy armour. At least their rounds were short, though. We'd watched them practicing the night before and it was the equivalent of an eight second ride on a bucking bull. I was very glad I hadn't chosen jousting as my sport. You were pretty much guaranteed to come crashing off your horse at least once per an event.

Everyone was excited and maybe a little nervous as we carefully groomed our horses and tacked them up.

We'd waited until the last minute to put our tunics on, so that they didn't get dirty, but once they were on we felt more like we fit in with our surroundings.

Somewhere outside a drum began to beat out a steady rhythm that sounded like a too-rapid heartbeat, and I took a deep breath and led Red outside.

"Ready?" Rob asked, grinning at me.

"Ready to beat your team? Yes I am." I laughed.

"Right, see you on the other side."

We all led our horses over to the makeshift ring that had been decorated with colourful streamers and banners. The bases and edges of our targets had been wrapped in cloth too that now fluttered in the breeze, making everything look very festive.

The order of go was that our least experienced team-members would go first since they would just be walking and trotting, and we'd move up toward the advanced riders as we progressed. We would alternate archers from each team until everyone had gone and then add up our points for the day. There would be a winning team announced for each of the three days but the final, official, score wouldn't be listed until Sunday at the very end.

It wasn't an official competition, of course, so we didn't have to follow any format for the targets. What we'd come up with was a mixture of a Hungarian and a Korean course and you were meant to shoot one just one arrow into each target. We had five targets in total. The first and the last targets were just flat squares meant to be shot at sideways when your horse was parallel to the them.

The three targets in the middle were positioned closely side by side with one target facing forward, one sideways and one backward. This meant that you had to change your position for almost every shot and, since you only had one arrow for each target, you had to think before you launched your arrow. If you missed the target there were no second chances.

Because of the setup in our field, we'd decided to have four riders do their runs and then wait down at the end of the field while the scores were tallied and the arrows pulled from the targets before riding back up to the top and having the next four riders go.

As expected, there were only a dozen or so spectators when we started. Which was just fine with me. The less people watching, the better. Both Ally and Logan's parents were there to cheer them on, and Logan's grandfather.

"All right, Ally. You've got this," I told her as she quietly walked Piper to the edge of the field. "Just take your time and don't worry about speed at all. Go at whatever pace you like."

Even though she'd managed to trot, and sometimes even canter, our archery course many times already it was still hard for her to coordinate both her own body and Piper's. Laszlo had told her that it was just fine for her to trot in and then walk if she needed the time to set up her shot properly. It wouldn't be allowed in a real competition but, at this stage in the game, it was more important that the riders have fun and a come away with a good experience rather than go too fast, miss all their shots, and just end up frustrated and unhappy.

"All right, for the blue team, we have our first rider up," the young guy who was our volunteer announcer said. He wore blue silks with a gold sash and a hat with a feather. I wasn't sure which time period he was supposed to be from but he looked like he could have stepped off of a Robin Hood movie set.

Ally looked pale but determined. She leaned forward to run her hand down Piper's neck a few times and then tightened her jaw, sat up straight, and urged the mare into an easy, almost shuffling, trot. Piper wasn't fast, but she was steady and trustworthy, and Ally was able to drop her reins and concentrate on taking careful aim at each target. Ally was a good archer. She'd been on the school team for years and had done a fair number of competitions by now. So as soon as she was able to just trust Piper and let go, the rest just fell into place.

The first two arrows landed with solid *thwunks* close to each bullseye, the third one went a little high and hit the very edge of the target and the fourth one, the backward shot, sailed somewhere off into the field to disappear into the grass. She composed herself enough to hit the final target and finished her ride with a big smile and another pat on Piper's neck.

"Good job!"

We all clapped, cheered, and whistled, and then it was Lincoln's turn, riding for the white team.

Although he was definitely not a natural rider, and he still wasn't completely confident on Whiskey, he had worked as hard as anyone this last week and he was riding to win.

He started off at a bumpy trot and then clucked Whiskey into a slow canter. The first shot went a bit wide, but he was ready for the second and third one, and he made the backward shot. But he leaned way too far to the side, causing Whiskey to drop into his jarring trot again and so the last shot flew off somewhere into the field.

Still, he patted Whiskey heartily when he pulled him to a stop and turned around to face us with a grin.

We went on like that, alternating back and forth, cheering for everyone no matter whose team they were on and groaning when shots were missed.

We cheered extra hard when Isabelle nimbly cantered the flighty little Pogo down the line without the mare spooking, stopping, or flinching even once.

There were more spectators gathered around the fence by the time the more advanced riders were ready to go.

I was right in the middle of the pack and I concentrated on having Red balanced beneath me, urging him into a gallop. A course like this was relatively easy for me since I didn't have weave between trees or shoot on any crazy angles, but Laszlo had been helping me to increase the speed with which I could draw my arrows from my quiver and shoot. And also to get used to Red going faster than a canter. We weren't used to doing too much actual galloping at home so having this straight course to just go full speed on had been really fun. Even on trustworthy Red, the gallop had felt a little intimidating at first so it had been my goal to slowly increase my speed.

"All right, Red," I whispered as soon as I hit the first target, "go for it."

He flattened his ears and put on another burst of speed, more than I was expecting, and I moved quickly, firing the arrows one by one with deadly precision.

I pulled him up at the end, breathing hard and grinning from ear to ear hearing the whoops and cheers of my teammates at the top of the hill. Red snorted loudly and actually pranced for a few steps, not ready to go from warhorse mode to quiet pony just yet.

"Easy there, buddy." I laughed and stroked his neck, admiring the effect of blue yarn that had been braided into his mane against his coppery coat. He really was a horse in a million.

Austin came behind me and I had to admit that he was riding much better than he had been at the start of the week. He certainly wasn't afraid of speed, and he had Kestrel flying down the course while he fired off his arrows in rapid succession.

"Good job," I congratulated him as soon as he pulled up.

"Thanks, you too. That horse looked fantastic. He has a real motor when he wants to use it."

"Kestrel did great, too," I said, trying to steer the conversation away from Red. I didn't like the way Austin was looking at him, like he wanted to push me off my horse and take him for himself.

"Yeah, I'm glad I rode her for this clinic. She's not as fast as what I'd like in a competition horse, but she's been fun. Now, you get one more chance to sell me that horse or there will be consequences."

He said it in such a casual voice that I didn't really take in what he'd said at first.

"Sorry, what?"

"You heard me." The smile was still on his face but he was looking at me coldly. "Go to your aunt, say you want to sell Red, and nobody will get hurt—"

He broke off suddenly as Mara came galloping toward us, Kitty moving faster than either of us had, eating up the ground as

Mara shot ruthlessly into the targets. Mara was whooping out loud as she rode, looking and sounding like a warrior princess.

I was too stunned to say anything and Austin moved Kestrel away and was congratulating Mara like nothing had happened at all. It almost felt like I'd dreamt it.

I'll have to tell someone what he said, I thought, *I have no idea what he meant but he sounded crazy. What if he hurts Red or one of the other horses?*

But there were more riders coming and Austin didn't try to speak to me again so gradually, I was caught up in the competition again and I almost forgot what had happened. Almost.

The morning finished successfully. We'd each had two rides through the course with varying success.

Nobody had fallen or embarrassed themselves too badly. No horses had bolted or crashed through the rope barrier. Everyone had been proud of their runs even if there were things to improve on, and the small crowd that had gathered had clapped when it was all over and it was announced that the white team had collected the most points of the morning.

"I loved that, but I'm so glad we're done for today," Ally said. "I'm exhausted."

We'd bathed the horses and put them away and then had made our way down to the makeshift village to grab snacks and homemade rock candy before heading back to the broodmare barn where our archery field had been transformed into an area for jousting.

"Me, too," I said, torn between watching the huge horses get ready and in scanning the area to see if I could see any sign of Portia.

She had bolted out of the stall as soon as I put Red away and the last I'd seen of her she'd been trundling off toward the back of the field. I didn't actually mind that she was out as long as she didn't get in anyone's way or get run over by a gigantic horse in armour.

All thoughts of Portia slipped my mind when the jousting began, though.

First, all the horses lined up together, and then their riders took them on a gallop around the upper part of the field, their footfalls shaking the earth when they passed by where we were sitting. The pounding of hooves mixed in with the beat of the heavy drums that had been set up alongside the ring until my heart pounded in my chest.

A trumpet blast started the show and the announcer, the same one that had helped us during the archery match, called the names of the horses and riders one by one. They too were divided into teams, red and blue, and they took turns charging at one another down a chute, their heavy lances pointed, aimed to either smash the armor of their opponent or send them flying right off their horses.

It was amazing and terrifying at the same time and I was super impressed by the bravery of both the horses and the riders.

After the match was over and the winner of the day was declared we headed back down to the range where Laszlo was giving archery demonstrations to any of the spectators who were interested.

The afternoon flew by in a whirl and it wasn't until it was time to feed the horses their dinner that I remembered about Portia.

"It's not like her to be missing so long," I told Rob worriedly, "she usually always comes back for dinner."

"Maybe she's down in the village," he said, meaning the makeshift vendor tents. "She likes food and it smells pretty good down there. And she likes people. She's probably hanging out with someone down there. I'll come with you to look if you like."

"Yeah, we'd better—" I broke off suddenly as Lillian's truck came bouncing down the short cut and skidded to a stop in front of the broodmare barn.

"Astrid," she said excitedly out the window, "you have visitors at the house. Jump in."

"What?" I looked at her in confusion and then suddenly realized what she meant. I'd actually almost forgot that my parents were coming. Now that they'd arrived, I felt almost faint with fear.

"Don't worry, I'll go look for Portia," Rob said. He paused, frowning. "Unless you want me to come with you instead. Do you need backup?"

"No, I guess I should do this on my own," I said with a heavy sigh. "Come back soon, though. I don't want to be left with them alone forever."

"You got this," Rob said, pulling me in a tight hug before pushing me toward the waiting truck. "I won't be long."

Aunt Lillian was humming under her breath when I climbed into the truck so I knew that she was nervous too. She always hummed when she was uncertain.

"You ready for this?" she asked bouncing up the rutted shortcut to the house.

"No, not really. How long are they staying?"

"Just the weekend. But they are headed to the coast afterward for a few weeks so they might try and see you again there. I'm just preparing you."

"Okay, thanks." *And so it begins,* I thought. "Have you seen the baby already?"

"Yes, she's adorable. She looks like you did when you were a baby, actually. Right now she has dark hair and blue eyes, but baby's change so much as they grow that who knows what she'll end up looking like."

"Does Marion seem … happy?" I asked uncertainly.

"I think so. She looks tired, which is pretty normal for a new mom. But I think she's more content then I've ever seen her."

I nodded and took a deep breath. I didn't bother asking about my dad. We were nearly at the house and I'd find out for myself soon enough.

My stomach churned as we pulled up in front of the big log building and I had to work hard to keep from throwing up. Most of the rest of the participants were out on lawn playing with croquet mallets in the near dusk and the air was filled with happy laughter. Something I definitely did not feel right then.

"You've got this, Astrid," Lillian said, echoing Rob's earlier words. "Just talk with them for a few minutes and then I'll call everyone in for dinner."

I've got this, I've got this, I repeated to myself as I walked up the stairs, opened the front door, and forced myself to turn to the sunken living where Aunt Lillian had left them drinking their tea.

And there they were, although for a second I hardly recognized them.

Marion looked thinner than I remembered. She'd always been tiny but now she was rail-thin and had dark circles around her eyes. But a smile lit up her tired face and Lillian had been right; she did look happy.

My dad looked even more different than Marion did. He'd grown a giant beard for one thing, and his lean frame that had been toned by hours of exercise had filled out a little and looked softer. His eyes still held the same sharp, commanding look, though. And even though his smile when he saw me was definitely genuine, I could see him sizing me up, judging, sorting, compartmentalizing me. Already finding me lacking before I'd even opened my mouth.

I stood, frozen in the doorway, the old feelings of panic warring with my new feelings of confidence. But it was the little figure in the basket on the couch between them that finally got my feet moving toward them.

"Astrid," Marion said, with real joy in her voice. "You look fantastic. It's is so, so good to see you."

She didn't get up and I went over and hugged her, my eyes still fixed on the impossibly tiny creature in the basket.

"Meet your sister, Aurora," Marion continued, her voice dropping to a whisper. "Meet your sister, Astrid."

The baby kept her eyes closed but she stretched a little and made a tiny little puckering motion with her mouth and instantly, I was completely in love.

"She's so tiny," I said, dropping my voice down low too so I didn't wake her up. "She's like a doll."

"She'll catch up soon enough," my dad said brusquely, startling me. "Good to see you, Astrid. I trust you are well."

"Yes, thank you," I said woodenly, dropping into the chair closest to Marion. "I hope you had a good trip."

"Oh, it's been lovely," Marion said, "we've always enjoyed going on road trips. We saw a huge herd of caribou crossing the road right as we were leaving."

We made small talk for the next few minutes while Aunt Lillian bustled around in the kitchen and then thankfully, she announced that it was time for dinner.

She made a place for Marion and my dad at the top of the table and the baby was kept in her basket off to the side.

"I hope you don't mind," Marion said blushing, "I'm not quite ready to leave her alone yet. We've had such a rough time."

"Of course not," Lillian reassured her. "She's welcome to sit right there. You let me know if you need anything at all."

The door slammed about ten times as everyone trooped in, laughing and jostling each other. There were so many people that we had to pull up extra chairs to the table and there was barely elbow room for everyone but it was a happy group, tired and satisfied from the morning's competition and eager to relive their stories from the day.

Rob came in last and I looked up hopefully, certain that he'd found Portia. But he just shook his head and took a spot at the end of the table.

Darn it, where could she be? I thought unhappily. *I hope she didn't wander away and get eaten by a wild animal.*

It was possible but unlikely. Technically there were bears, cougars, and wolves around but there was so much noise and activity around right now that I doubted any predators would be prowling near the barns. The most likely thing was that she'd been locked in one of the barns somewhere. She'd probably gotten into one of the hay storage sheds and was happily eating. I would have to do another search after dinner.

I knew that down at the tent village they were doing the first night of their pig roast. There would be lots of people around who would have noticed a sheep trotting loose. Somebody would have seen her.

I broke out of my thoughts when I heard my name being spoken across the table.

"Your daughter has been a delight to have as part of the clinic," Laszlo was saying to my father. He looked like he was a few cups into the wine. His cheeks were red and he was beaming at my dad like he was a long-lost friend. "She is hard-working and talented, as are all the students here, but she in particular would fit in very well at my stable in Hungary. I do have a working student position available but of course, it's a long way to go and of course, her parents would have to be on board."

What? I stared at him incredulously wondering why on earth he hadn't mentioned this to me earlier. Of course he couldn't know that I hadn't talked to my estranged parents in over a year and that they knew very little about what I liked and wanted in life.

"Well, that's a great offer," my dad was saying, "we could consider it. Would it be a paid position or would she be working for free?"

"Whoa, whoa, whoa," Aunt Lillian said suddenly, cutting this little negotiation session off before it could get started. "Let's back the train up here. Astrid isn't going to *Hungary* by herself, she's still a child and she has a life on the Island. If she's going anywhere it would be to live permanently at the ranch here. Goodness knows I've invited her to stay enough times."

"I'm still her father, Lillian," my dad warned her, raising his voice. "I think I know what's best for—"

From beside the table, baby Aurora began to cry, a soft wailing sound like a cat calling.

"I'll take care of her," Marion said, standing up and swooping the basket into her arms. She disappeared in the direction of their bedroom without a backward glance.

"Thanks for dinner, Aunt Lillian," I said, standing up abruptly. "I've got to go and find Portia, she's missing."

From across the table, Austin looked up and met my gaze, a wicked gleam in his eye.

"That's too bad," he said in his smooth voice. "Guess you should have kept a better eye on her. Hope she didn't fall in the *river* or anything."

"Astrid, sit down," my dad ordered, "we're not done discussing this. Mr. Belko has made you a generous offer."

Rob stood up, his eyes fixed on my dad, and I pushed back my chair and headed toward the door.

The night air felt good on my hot face and I took a deep breath as soon as I hit the porch.

Rob appeared beside me, taking my hand in his and together we walked down toward the barn.

"That was intense," he said finally.

"It always is," I said grimly. "A year away from them wasn't nearly long enough. We need to find Portia, though. I think Austin locked her somewhere. He's still mad that I didn't sell him Red. I hope he didn't hurt her, though."

"You don't think he'd do that, do you? I mean he's spoiled but he seems all right."

"I'm not sure. Sometimes he seems okay, and then it's like this other side of him comes out. He said something weird today when we were riding, something about it being my last chance to sell Red or he'd make me pay."

"Okay, that's creepy. Why didn't you tell me that earlier?"

"I don't know." I shrugged. "There was a lot going on. I forgot. But the way, the way he looked at dinner makes me think that he's up to something."

We gave the horses their late night flakes of hay and went carefully from paddock to paddock looking for any sign of Portia.

We checked the hay room and the tack room, and then went out back to walk the pasture. We didn't see her in the dim glow from our headlamps but it was a big pasture and it was possible that we might have missed her.

"We'll check again when it's light out," Rob said, squeezing my hand reassuringly.

We walked down to the training barn, calling her name every few minutes and listening hard for her distinctive *baa*. I held my breath when we got to the bridge crossing the river, remembering what Austin had said at the table. Would he have really have pushed her in?

I shone my light all over the bridge and into the water below but there was no sign of a struggle and no sign of Portia.

"Could she have gone up to find the other sheep?" Rob asked.

"Maybe, but I don't see why. She's never shown any interest in them before and they're so far from here."

We checked the training barn thoroughly and the paddocks, and then we wandered to the cluster of tents where a loud and somewhat drunken pig-roast was in full swing. There was lots of singing and banging of mugs on the long tables that had been set up. We asked a few people on the outskirts of the party if anyone had seen her but nobody had.

"We'll keep looking in the morning," Rob said sympathetically. "We might have better luck when it's light out."

"I feel so bad. I should have watched her more closely. I should have been looking after her."

"We'll find her," Rob said kindly.

By the time we got back to the house, Marion and the baby were in bed and my dad was in the living room having some in-depth conversation about Alaska with Bruce and Isabelle. I managed to slip by unnoticed and crept up to my room to be alone.

I lay in bed staring at the ceiling wondering why on earth my life was always so complicated.

CHAPTER 27

The next morning I was up before dawn and the first thing on my mind was finding Portia.

I crept down the stairs and was surprised to find that both Aunt Lillian and Laszlo were in the kitchen already, talking quietly over coffee at the big table.

"Oh, Astrid, you're up early. You must have known we were talking about you."

"You were?" I said nervously, going to the coffee pot to fill my travel mug.

"I must apologize for that scene last night, Astrid," Laszlo said. "I had no idea about your complicated family relations. I really put my foot in things."

"It's okay," I said, smiling at him. "You couldn't have known."

"My offer still stands if you want it, of course. I do take on working students every year."

"It's tempting," I said honestly, "but I don't want to leave home yet. I'm not ready. I feel like I'm just getting settled for the first time in my life. I don't want to lose what I've built."

"That's very mature of you," Laszlo said approvingly. "I wish

I'd been as together as you are when I was your age. I was a bit haywire."

"No way," I said, laughing. "I can't picture that."

"Oh, I was wild. My poor parents had no idea what to do with me. I'm afraid that I was a bit spoiled and more than a little arrogant, too. Young Austin actually reminds me of me in my younger years."

"No, he's not nice like you are, at all," I said, seeing absolutely nothing similar between the two of them.

"Well, sometimes compassion and kindness comes with age and experience. Not everyone is born with that like you are. Some of us have to have our characters developed by a lifetime of bad choices."

"Speaking of bad choices," I said. "Portia is still missing and I'm sure Austin has something to do with it. Can you talk to him for me? He's still mad that I wouldn't let Aunt Lillian sell him Red."

"Oh for pity's sake, really?" Aunt Lillian said. "He was disappointed when I told him no, but I thought he understood."

"No, he was really mad. He said he would make me pay if he didn't get Red."

"Well, why on earth am I just hearing about this now?" my aunt said in astonishment. "Nobody is allowed to *threaten* you, Astrid. Nobody."

"I thought I could handle it," I said with a shrug. "I didn't know he really meant it. But now with Portia missing—"

"I will talk to him," Laszlo said. "We will find your sheep."

Even though the sun was hardly up, Rob and Nori were already down at the barn working on cleaning the paddocks.

"Don't worry, we're going to help you find her," Nori said, coming over to give me an unexpected hug. "Mara's coming, too."

But it wasn't just Mara who came down the steps to the loft, it was all the other riders, too. And then Bruce and Isabelle and

Jessie and John came out of their tents, fully dressed and ready to help.

"We heard that your pet is missing, Astrid," Bruce said. "We won't stop looking until she's found."

"Oh, you don't have to do that," I said quickly, "you have to ride in a few hours. I don't want you to miss—"

"Don't you worry about that," he said firmly. "Let's just start looking."

"A bunch of us are going to ride up to the upper pastures and check if she's headed out to be with the sheep flock. If she started making her way there we should be able to find her. There are a bunch of gates in between here and there so she wouldn't have been able to make it too far." Mara looked at me kindly.

"Thank you so much," I said, "that means a lot."

After the riders left, the rest of us combed the big archery field again until we were positive that Portia wasn't there. Then we walked down to the training barn again, scouring the sides of the road, the bridge and the river, but there was no sign of her. We checked the training barn again, going over every nook and cranny to make sure we hadn't overlooked her.

"Let's check the village one more time. The tent village was pretty quiet that early in the morning but there were a few people wandering around setting up the displays and cleaning up from last night's party.

"Yes, I did see her trotting around here," said the woman who ran the candy tent. "She was playing with some kids, I think. Some guy was trying to round her up, though. He kept trying to catch her but she's faster than she looks, I guess."

"Did you see where they went?" I asked eagerly, glad for any sort of lead.

"No, sorry. I only saw them for a minute or so. That was in the late afternoon."

"Okay, great, thanks."

"See, we'll find her," Rob said, smiling. "We're getting close."

We searched the tents one by one until only the big food tent was left. It still smelled like ale and burnt pig around the pit of coals.

"Oh, my gosh, Rob," I said, clutching his arm. "There's her collar."

I ran forward and snatched it up, looking around wildly as if she would appear out of nowhere.

"What's this shed for?" Rob asked cautiously, looking at the plastic shed door that had a lock on it.

"I'm not sure, let's see if we can find anyone to open it."

There was nobody around though, or at least nobody who had a key.

"It's just plastic," Nori said, "we can pop the hinges off easily, can't we?"

"I suppose," Rob said with a sigh, "come on, you two, help me."

We all grasped the left side of the double door and on the count of three we pulled as hard as we could. With a cracking pop, the door fell toward us and we set it to the ground.

"Oh, Astrid, don't look," Nori wailed.

I only had a second to take in the familiar shaped white body and the vacant eyes before I began to scream.

"It's okay," Rob said, grabbing me to keep from bolting. "Calm down, it's not her. Astrid, it's not Portia. It's the pig. It's the pig for the dinner tonight. You're okay, open your eyes. It's not her."

It took me a minute to really hear what he was saying and when I finally opened my eyes, a feeling of rage poured over me.

It wasn't Portia, no matter what my mind had told me when I'd first opened the door, it was just the poor body of the pig resting in its pool of ice, getting ready for that night's dinner. But someone had wrapped the lower half of it in a white tarp and drawn a skull and cross bones in marker on it. A black arrow had been stabbed through the tarp, right into the pig. Which was creepy and also probably not very hygienic.

"I'm going to kill him," I said fiercely. "I am seriously going to—"

"Okay, let's find her first, then we'll kill him."

"Wait," Nori said, "have we actually checked the archery range yet? Maybe that arrow is a clue."

We hurried across the road and I gingerly pushed open the front door, hoping against hope.

"Yes, she's been here!" Nori cried, as we stopped to look at the destruction inside. The whole room had been turned upside down, bows and arrows knocked to the floor and the floor scattered with smeared sheep manure.

"Portia?"

I was greeted with an indignant *baa* as Portia trotted out of the bathroom, trailing a roll of toilet paper from her mouth.

"Oh my gosh, Portia. You're alive." I knelt down right on the filthy floor and wrapped my arms around her, bursting into happy tears. She nuzzled her nose against my cheek and then pulled back, reaching down to search my pockets for treats.

"You poor thing, you must have been starving," I said, buckling her collar safely back in place.

"It looks like he left a bucket of water for her in the bathroom and there are bits of hay in there. I think he fed her a bit," Nori said.

"That doesn't make him much less of a monster," I said angrily. "She was probably terrified. Come on, Portia, let's get you back to your stall."

The riders were just returning when we got back and they all let out a cheer when they saw that Portia had been safely found.

I didn't get to see Laszlo's conversation with Austin after he heard about what had happened to Portia and about the destruction of the archery range. All I knew is that Austin didn't get to ride with us in the tournament that afternoon and that he was nowhere to be seen until dinner time.

I was kept busy between riding, helping my teammates get

ready, and avoiding my dad and Marion as much as I could. This was easy enough with Marion since she would pretty much stay wherever she was parked—the edge of the ring, the dinner table, the barn aisle—and just stare lovingly down at Aurora as if she didn't even notice anything else going on around her. It was like they were a tiny island of two and nobody else existed.

I'd heard my dad cheering me on when I did my runs. And I'd overheard him chatting happily enough with the other archers. But we hadn't been alone together for more than a minute.

"They came all this way to see you, dear," Aunt Lillian said quietly, "you should spend a little more time with them."

"But I don't know what to say when I'm around them," I confessed to her. "And I don't think they actually care about the same things that I do. I don't think they really know me at all."

Lillian had sighed and patted me on the shoulder, but she hadn't argued.

"No, you're probably right. But at least they care enough to be here."

That was true. And I did like seeing baby Aurora even though she looked like a tiny alien. She had huge eyes when she was awake enough to open them and her fixed stare seemed to look right into my soul.

"I think she likes you, Astrid," Marion had told me, "she knows you're her big sister who will always look out for her."

"Yeah," I said, smiling down at Aurora's solemn little face. "I guess I would look out for her."

Austin wasn't at dinner either, and I was startled, and happy, to see him slowly lugging his belongings out to his oversized car.

I hadn't intended to say anything to him before he left, but when I went outside, he was sitting on the porch swing looking thoughtfully off into the woods.

"I wanted to talk to you," he said quickly, before I could duck back into the house. "I'm leaving tonight but I wanted to apologize first."

"Okay," I said warily.

"I'm sorry I scared you and that I locked up Portia. I wouldn't have really hurt her, but I know you didn't know that. It was really mean of me."

Startled, I felt tears prickling my eyes.

"And I shouldn't have messed with you about Red. I knew you wouldn't sell him. Heck, I didn't even really want him. It's just that sometimes when I see a challenge, it's like I can't back down from it. I just have to keep pushing until I get what I want."

"Um, that's pretty messed up."

"Yeah, I know. I'm working on it. I made your aunt an offer on Kestrel, too."

"You did? I thought she wasn't flashy enough for you."

"She's a good horse. Laszlo says I should take this year to work on my position and form so that's what I'll do, I guess. And she'll be good company for Iggy while he recovers. My sister wants to try horse archery too, and Kestrel would be a good match for her once I move on."

"Well, that sounds, uh, nice."

"Your aunt said she wouldn't sell her to me unless you agreed to it."

"She did?" I asked in surprise.

"Yep, so what do you think?"

I shrugged and looked away. Austin was not the best person in the world, but he cared for his horse and he had improved a lot as a rider over the last week. And Kestrel did need a home. How many more chances like this would she get? It was probably better than going to the auction.

"Fine," I said, "but you'd better take good care of her."

"Right, I will. Thank you." He stood up and reached out his hand for me to shake. "Goodbye, Astrid. Right now you're a better rider than me and a better archer. I look forward to getting good enough to beat you someday."

"Bye, Austin," I said, watching for a moment while he strode toward his Hummer and hopped in.

"You think there's hope for him?" Rob said, pushing open the screen door to stand beside me.

"Um, maybe? Hard to tell. I have the feeling we'll be seeing him again one day."

"Oh, why's that?"

"I don't know. Just a feeling."

CHAPTER 28

My dad waited until the next morning, just as I was beginning to warm Red up for the last day of our tournament, before trying to break the ice with me.

I'd seen him standing nearby but I'd been too focused trying to keep half an eye on Ally and Lincoln who were trotting in circles around the far end of the pasture and concentrate on Red's warm up that I hadn't really given him much thought.

"Keep your head in the game, Astrid," he said suddenly, appearing at my side.

"Sorry, what?" I'd just stopped Red for a second so I could watch Isabelle canter by on Pogo. The little mare had spotted a fluttering banner and her head had shot up. She'd definitely thought about bolting but Isabelle had kept her calmly in hand.

"You're losing focus. You're thinking about what others are doing and not yourself."

"Ah, thanks, Dad. I know that. But it's not actually about me today. I'm here to help the others, too. Some of these guys are beginners. I'm sort of half-working at this clinic."

"Hmph," he said, looking at the ground. "Well, when you get

to Hungary, I suppose that will be your time to shine then. Then you can put the focus on your own career."

I stared down at him, at his shining eyes and the possessive hand he'd laid on Red's neck.

He's just trying to live his own dreams through me, I thought suddenly, *this has nothing to do with what I want at all.*

"I'm not going to Hungary, Dad", I said firmly, "not now and maybe not ever."

"Well, that's ridiculous, Astrid. You've been handed an opportunity here. You have to take it."

"I really don't. I have a life back on the Island. And I have Rob. And I have Red, Portia, and Caprice to take care of."

"Pets are replaceable," he said angrily. "And how many childish, high school romances do you think actually last? You're throwing away your career for some boy you won't probably even see again once you graduate. And a horse, a dog, and a barnyard animal are hardly an excuse not to go. Those are childish attachments that should be put aside."

I stared at him steadily, watching the frustration and anger flicker across his face. His cheeks were flushed and his eyes glittered brightly and I suddenly realized that none of his rage really had anything to do with me at all. It had never been about me, or Marion, or the things that went wrong in his workplace. It was something that lived inside of him, an illness really, ready to ignite over the slightest thing.

He's just like Austin, I thought in surprise. *When things are out of his control, he freaks out and has to bully everyone around him until he feels better.*

"Why are you looking at me like that?" he demanded.

"Because I'm not afraid of you anymore," I said calmly. "I was so worried about seeing you again, but now I realize that it doesn't matter. You have no power over me at all. You have nothing to hurt me with."

"I don't want to hurt you, Astrid," he said, looking shocked. "I just want what's best for you."

"No, maybe you think that's the truth but it's not. I never knew what family was growing up, but now I do. It's people who care about you, and who have your back, no matter what. And now that I've figured that out, I'm going to hold on to those people as tightly as I can. That means Rob and Aunt Lillian and the Ahlbergs. And I know you won't understand this, but it also means Red, Caprice and yes, a stupid sheep who honestly has shown me more affection in the last year than you gave me in my entire life. And that means that I don't just abandon them without a second thought.

"That's what love is, Dad; you put others needs in front of your own sometimes. Not all the time, but in the moments where it counts."

He stared at me and I saw the anger drain out of his face, leaving him pale and ashy looking. Slowly he unclenched his fists and then took a deep sigh.

"Astrid, you're right, I'm sorry—"

"Okay," I said. "But Dad, I'm not going to let you affect my life like this anymore. And, you probably don't want to hear this, but you need to get your anger in check before your *other* daughter spends her whole childhood being terrified of you, too. You don't want to make the same mistake again."

We stared at each other for a moment, and then I patted Red and moved him off toward where Lincoln and Ally were still trotting in circles.

I didn't look back and every step I took away from him felt better than the last. I moved Red into a trot and then a loose canter, leaving the reins on his neck and letting him find the way.

CHAPTER 29

I managed to put everything out of my head for the rest of the competition. And, despite all the chaos that had happened to me in the last twenty-four hours, I somehow felt great and our runs were faster and more accurate than they'd ever been. Red was finding a whole set of new gears and I had to concentrate hard to keep up with the higher speeds.

In the end, it was the white team that won, but it didn't matter. We all had a great time and the spectators were entertained and everyone came away from it feeling happy with their runs. We'd come a very long way in just a week. Especially since some of the horses and riders had never seen a bow in their lives up until recently. Just being able to compete at all was an accomplishment.

My parents didn't say much more than to congratulate me and admire Red. My dad didn't mention our conversation again and the next morning, they packed up early and headed off.

"It was so nice to see you again, darling," Marion said, smiling at me dreamily. "I'm so glad you got to meet your sister."

"She's beautiful, Marion," I said honestly. "I'm really glad she's going to be okay."

"And maybe you can visit us in Alaska someday. We'd love to show you the sights."

"Er, maybe," I said. "Thanks."

"Take care of yourself, Astrid," my father said, slapping me jovially on the shoulder like I was another player on the squash court. "Good luck with everything and don't be a stranger."

"Right, see you next time," I said because I knew that there could actually be a next time. I didn't have to panic anymore at the thought of seeing them. I could see them once a year and keep an eye on how Aurora was doing and not have to feel any fear, guilt, or remorse anymore. That part of my life was officially over.

CHAPTER 30

Saying goodbye to Mr. Belko and the rest of the archery participants was harder than saying goodbye to my own parents.

We'd only been together a week, but I felt like I'd known them all for years.

"I hope you will all consider joining me in Hungary in years to come," Laszlo said, "there is plenty of time and you are always welcome."

"We'd better see you out there competing soon," Riley said, giving me a tight hug. "You need to bring an Island team with you to the next meet."

"We're going to start our own horse archery club," Nori said, which was news to me. "I've got it all planned out."

I looked at the innocent smile on her face, wondering what she was up to. Nori had a way of barging ahead with half-baked plans and dragging me along with her.

"Don't be a stranger," Bruce said. "You guys can come visit us whenever you like."

There was lots of hugging and laughing and exchanging email

addresses and phone numbers and, just like that, everyone had departed and we were alone.

It was strange, and a little sad to go down to the training barn and see it without the backdrop of the makeshift village, everything looked plain and less festive.

"Oh well, I guess it's back to business as usual," Aunt Lillian said with a sigh. "I never would have thought I would enjoy the festival so much, but it was actually a hit. Those dress-up people were very nice. And you kids did an amazing job getting everything organized. There is no way I could have done it without you. I really don't know how to repay you."

"You don't need to do anything for us," I said quickly. "We had a great time. It was an amazing opportunity. I almost don't want to go home."

"Well, I was hoping you'd say that actually," Aunt Lillian began.

I sighed, knowing she was going to ask me to stay there and live with her for about the millionth time.

"I have a proposition for you kids."

I glanced at Rob and Nori who stared at her expectantly.

"I'd like you to stay here for another month and work for me. I promise to make it worth your while. I would like to get those ranch horses out of here as fast as I can and they'd do better at auction if they were going solidly under saddle again. I'm not as callous as you think, Nori. I want to find good homes for them, too."

Nori blushed and looked quickly down at the ground.

"And Rob, I know you didn't get all the lessons with Liza that you were hoping to, so I propose that we get Allan to bring your fancy dressage horse up for the month so you can get some proper work done."

"Oh, wow," Rob said, looking startled. "I'd have to check with my dad but yeah, that sounds great. Thank you."

"Well, I can definitely stay," Nori said. "I'm in no hurry to get back. But I guess I'll call my mom and tell her that I'm not coming home yet."

"Well, that's considerate of you, dear." My aunt laughed. "I'm sure she'd love to hear from you."

She turned to look at me expectantly.

"Of course I'd love to. I just have to check with Earl and the Ahlbergs to make sure they can spare me." For some reason I suddenly thought of Oona's painting waiting for me back at the farm and felt a pang of homesickness that I quickly pushed away. The painting could wait; it wasn't like I was staying here forever.

"Well that's settled then. Oh, and Astrid, I almost forgot, this is for you."

"What is it?" I said, staring down at the large, cream-coloured envelope with a familiar logo in the upper corner.

"Oh, just a little something I wanted you to have. I was going to wait for your birthday, but I guess you might as well have it now."

"Well, open it," Nori said when I just stared down at the envelope.

But I didn't have to open it. I already knew what was inside. Still, I fumbled with the flap, peered inside and then threw myself at Aunt Lillian with a choking sob, burying my face in her shoulder as she hugged me hard.

"He's all yours, sweetheart. One hundred percent yours."

And later that night, I put Red's newly framed registration certificate, with my name officially printed on the back, right on the desk beside my bed where I could look at it whenever I wanted.

Far off in the woods I heard the familiar, mournful call of the owl. First one hooting by itself and then another answering call from closer to the house. It didn't send shivers of dread down my spine like it had in the past. Maybe the owl represented change but I knew now that change didn't have to be a bad thing. It could be a wonderful, magical thing, too.

And now a whole other month of freedom stretched out in front of me. A whole month of riding and shooting surrounded by the people and horses that I loved. And it meant spending time with my best friend in the world, my very own Red.

The End

MORE READING AND RESOURCES

If you are enjoying the Defining Gravity series, The October Horses series or any of my other books, I'd love if you'd take a moment to write a review on any of the platforms where they are sold.

The October Horses series

The October Horses

Defining Gravity series

Defining Gravity

Flight

Freefall

Riding Above Air

Short Stories and Collections

The Horses of Winter

Greystone Manor mystery series (under G.M. Mckay)

The Curse of the Golden Touch

The Sting of the Serpent's Blade

The Wayfarer's End Series

The Opposite of Living

Good Bones

Wayfarer'sEnd

Visit my website at www.genevievemckay.com

Follow on Twitter @Geners_Mckay

Follow my pics on Instagram: @mckaygenevieve

Or join my Facebook author page: www.facebook.com/authorgenevievemckay

Are you interested in learning more about Classical Dressage? Visit Sylvia Loch's Classical Riding Club (http://www.classicalriding.co.uk) for links, videos, articles and books to help you improve your position, connection and relationship with your horse. It's free to join and anyone is welcome no matter what their riding level; it's all about learning. There are even online tests and lessons you can do from the comfort of home.

Some of my favourite non-fiction horse books are; The Classical Rider by Sylvia Loch, Centered Riding by Sally Swift, That Winning Feeling by Jane Savoie, The Complete Training of Horse and Rider by Alois Podhajsky and Dressage for the New Age by Dominique Barbier. There are so many more. Do you have a favourite training book to recommend?

Are you interested in learning more about Horseback Archery? The International Horseback Archery Alliance has links to organizations in various countries as well as postal matches where you can compete from home and send in your scores. https://www.horsebackarchery.info/links

ACKNOWLEDGMENTS

Acknowledgments

Huge thanks to my editor, Jinxie Gervasio, for being my first reader and for all the good advice.

Massive appreciation to Helen Cartwright, Helen Yeo, Honey Johnston, Marti Oltmann and the rest of the Advanced Reading team. Your help is invaluable!

Fabulous cover design credit goes to *Cover Design by James, GoOnWrite.com*

Big thanks to all the wonderful horses who I've met over the years. My journey with horses is a never-ending learning experience. I wouldn't have it any other way.

ABOUT THE AUTHOR

Genevieve is the author of eleven books and numerous short stories. She lives on the wild West Coast with her family which also includes horses, dogs, cats, sheep and chickens. She loves all types of riding and all breeds and types of horses, especially the quirky ones.

You can check out her website:

www.genevievemckay.com

Or visit the following Facebook and Instagram pages

facebook.com/authorgenevievemckay

instagram.com/mckaygenevieve

www.ingramcontent.com/pod-product-compliance
Lightning Source LLC
LaVergne TN
LVHW041154150826
845673LV00001B/160

* 9 7 8 1 7 7 7 1 3 6 9 1 8 *